Psychoanalysis
and
Psychopathology

Psychoanalysis and Psychopathology

PHILIP S. HOLZMAN

JASON ARONSON INC.
Northvale, New Jersey
London

THE MASTER WORK SERIES

First softcover edition 1995

Library of Congress Cataloging-in-Publication Data

Holzman, Philip S., 1922-
[Psychoanalysis and psychopathology]
An outline of Freud's ideas and their evolution / by Philip S. Holzman.
p.   cm.
Originally published under title: Psychoanalysis and
psychopathology : New York, McGraw-Hill, 1969.
Includes bibliographical references and index.
ISBN 1-56821-588-6 (alk. paper)
1. Psychoanalysis. 2. Psychology, Pathological. I. Title.
RC504.H66   1995
616.89'17—dc20   95-15115

Manufactured in the United States of America. Jason Aronson Inc. offers books and cassettes. For information and catalog write to Jason Aronson Inc., 230 Livingston Street, Northvale, New Jersey 07647.

To Ann, Natalie, Carl, and Paul

Editor's Introduction

One of the most significant dialogues in the history of science occurred in November 1882 when Josef Breuer related to Sigmund Freud the startling modifications in behavior that he had induced in Anna O., a young patient victimized by an overwhelming number of apparent somatic symptoms.

Breuer's recital of his cathartic method for removing these multiple disturbances eventually served as the stimulus for Freud's development of the whole range of psychoanalytic methods that became the first great weapons of science for overcoming the ravaging effects of behavior disorder. These early theoretical constructions remain historical landmarks for comprehending the etiology of neurosis.

Dr. Holzman has wisely seen fit to focus on this early period of the Freudian epoch, giving it the extended treatment it deserves. Beginning with a discussion of the intellectual forebears of psychoanalysis, the author then traces Freud's clinical observations as well as his first gropings to fit a theory to his data. Dr. Holzman has provided a description of disturbance and defense as Freud perceived them, and of the clinical material that produced the first theory of neurotic personality development, as well as of the disappointment which this theory subsequently engendered in its creator. In this volume the student will find a statement in depth of the later and more profound conceptualizations that first changed the face of psychiatry and later the orientation of all society. Dr. Holzman has included too a description of Freud's "Project for a Scientific Psychology": his construction of a neurological theory of the mind (a theory that is too often neglected by those interested in a scholarly appraisal of psychoanalysis). The author has not ignored current developments in psychoanalysis, for he concludes with an appraisal of the contributions of other major contemporary psychoanalytic theorists who have followed Freud's path.

This is not a simplistic book. Professor Holzman has not sought to compromise the reader by writing a treatise that defines the scope and breadth of psychoanalysis in narrow, popular terms. Instead, he has provided, in exemplary detail, a scholarly understanding of the relationship of psychoanalytic theory to psychopathology. This volume, intended for students, is an extension of Professor Holzman's efforts to provide for psychologists and psychiatrists a greater comprehension of the role of psychoanalytic theory in understanding disordered personality processes.

Philip Holzman occupies a unique position in American psychology. Trained in clinical psychology in the post-World War II years, he is the product of an early and unique amalgam of training in the fundamentals of experimental psychology (at the University of Kansas) and in sophisticated clinical understanding (at the Menninger Foundation in Topeka). During the years that followed his doctoral training, Dr. Holzman remained at the Menninger Clinic, cast in the multiple roles of researcher, clinical psychologist, and (after training in the Topeka Institute of Psychoanalysis) psychoanalyst and training analyst. His subsequent research studies of cognitive styles, perception, and self-confrontation (the effects of listening to one's own voice) have provided him with a focus for integrating psychoanalytic theory, experimental methodology, and personality research. Currently he is Professor of Psychoanalysis in the Department of Psychiatry, School of Medicine, University of Chicago, with a joint professorial appointment in the Department of Psychology. He retains his status as a training psychoanalyst in the Chicago Psychoanalytic Institure, and holds membership in the Chicago Psychoanalytic Society.

Numbered among Professor Holzman's mentors are many seminal figures. Exchanges with Gardner Murphy and Martin Scheerer strongly influenced his thinking in the areas of dynamic psychology, personality theory, and the interaction of perceptual processes and personality disposition. Clinical and research training with David Rapaport, George Klein, Robert Holt, Rudolf Ekstein, and Kark Menninger broadened that substantial psychological base.

There are some who, under the impact of the current Zeitgeist toward a more Skinnerian psychology, look to the construction of theories of psychopathology that can ignore the great theoretical constructs of psychoanalysis. Preoccupied with frustrations induced by a long-term failure to find the causes of mental illness, we frequently lose sight of the fact that Freud invigorated a psychiatric tradition troubled and enervated by a century of failure of attempts to derive from physiology, anatomy, and pathology answers to questions regarding the nature of mental disease. It seems unlikely that a radical behaviorism can be exempt from the lessons of history. Freud produced a vision that broke new ground for the observation and comprehension of behavior pathology. Perhaps the words of E. G. Boring in his classic *History of Experimental Psychology* (1950, p. 743) can best provide a historical context for reading Professor Holzman's book:

> In the first place, let it be said that the history of psychology is its past. The great men who were in it stand by whatever their influence was eventually to be. . . . So Freud. Psychologists long refused him admission to their numbers, yet now he is seen as the greatest originator of all, the agent of the Zeitgeist who accomplished the invasion of psychology by the principle of the unconscious process. If the author were to pick out psychology's great, in order to satisfy the reader's curiosity, then he would say that, judged by the criterion of their persistent posthumous importance, there are at least four very great men in psychology's history: Darwin, Helmholtz, James and Freud. Measured by the same criterion, Darwin and Freud have produced a greater revolution in thinking than have Helmholtz and James. Freud's effect is, however, still too recent to compare with Darwin's. For that we must wait fifty years.

Professor Holzman's volume will facilitate that perspective by analyzing the magnitude of Freud's contributions to the study of psychopathology.

Norman Garmezy

Consulting Editor

Preface to the New Edition

Freudian psychoanalysis represents a revolutionary change in the way we think about ourselves and about the nature of human nature. From its earliest beginnings, it has spurred us to ask questions not asked before about our psychological lives, questions that touch on the psychobiological motives for human behavior, the nature of conscience, the scope and limits of conscious thought. In these respects psychoanalysis occupies a major place in the history of ideas.

Twenty-five years ago I offered this small book to students as a systematic guide through the complex psychological theories of Sigmund Freud. It has been received as such. My emphasis was to clarify the body of formulations that made up psychoanalytic theory as Freud promulgated it. In that effort I tried to show that Freud constantly altered his formulations, indicating that they were to be regarded as continually developing rather than as fixed dogma. The book made no claim to completeness, inasmuch as it did not discuss Freud's psychoanalytic therapy or his social, anthropological, and literary works, which can claim equal time for discussion. But those aspects rest upon the formulations discussed in this book.

The book has been out of print for about a decade and I thank Jason Aronson, who has seen enough merit in it to republish it. Most authors, in rereading what they had written a quarter century ago, would want to revise their text. And there are several places in this text that I, too, would change, but these are mostly in interpretation of some events and not in the exposition of the theories and their modifications. They therefore should be left unmodified.

During the past two decades, arguments have continued to be joined about the scientific status of Freud's theories, to the benefit of all concerned. All formulations are imperfect and need to have their errors exposed. In my opinion, the principal weakness of psychoanalysis as a discipline lies in its isolation from academic institutions of higher learning. This "quarantine" has kept the richest yields of psychoanalysis from directly entering into the new era of cognitive explorations by test and experiment. Perhaps the reissue of this book can help to end that quarantine, and allow the richness of psychoanalysis to nurture the empirical thrust of new research.

Philip S. Holzman
Cambridge, Massachusetts
March 12, 1995

Preface

In spite of the wide influence of psychoanalysis on contemporary psychiatry and psychology, and the extraordinary way in which aspects of psychoanalysis have become assimilated into our culture, there are few helpful guides through its labyrinthine complexities besides the heroic task of perusing the complete works of Sigmund Freud. *Psychoanalysis and Psychopathology* is meant to serve as such a guide. It has been written primarily for students of psychology, both graduate and undergraduate, in order to provide them with a textbook that can be used to supplement class discussions as well as other textbooks on psychoanalysis. Medical students, psychiatric residents, and perhaps beginning candidates in psychoanalytic institutes may also find this book helpful.

Psychoanalysis and Psychopathology provides a historical sketch of Freud's psychoanalytic ideas and describes the evolution of the theories from the earliest clinical data through the several revisions and emendations required by new data and by intrinsic defects in the theories. It also includes some later additions to the corpus of the theory. However, it makes no claim to completeness, for such an enterprise would be encyclopedic and thus surely beyond the purview of a small supplementary text. For example, the discussion of the theory of instinctual drives all but neglects a discussion of Freud's last "dual instinct theory." Further, I have deliberately omitted a discussion of psychoanalytic treatment and technique and, thus, of considerations of such key concepts as "transference" and "countertransference." Nor have I included a discussion of Freud's social and anthropological papers, nor of his writings on applied psychoanalysis. I have also bypassed an examination of theories—such as those of Alfred Adler, Carl Jung, Otto Rank, Karen Horney, Erich Fromm, Harry Stack Sullivan, and Melanie Klein—that began from a Freudian psychoanalytic base but branched away from classical psychoanalytic concerns in some significant ways.

Although I have deliberately limited the range of psychoanalytic subjects, I have tried to present the fundamental substantive psychological issues in psychoanalysis as understandably as possible without oversimplifying them to the point of misrepresenting them. To some readers, the results of this effort may appear to be unduly complex and demanding. I hope that most readers will find the effort worth their while and that they will be encouraged to go to the primary sources for further elaboration.

As an aid to understanding, a simple glossary is provided at the end of the book. While it is by no means complete, an attempt was made to include most of the special words used in this book in reference to psychoanalysis.

I have adopted a uniform bibliographic reference to Freud's psychoanalytic writings: the excellent new translation by James and Alix Strachey. This 24-volume set, *The Standard Edition of the Complete Psychological Works of Sigmund Freud,* is unsurpassed in clarity and completeness. The reader who wants to go more deeply into the subject of psychoanalysis will be rewarded by referring to these volumes with their copious and clarifying notes.

At the editor's suggestion I have included short, skeletal summaries at the end of each chapter except Chapter 11, which itself is a summary statement of the book.

Many people have contributed to this book. The influence of David Rapaport, who was my teacher, is pervasive, and I acknowledge my great debt to him. Twenty-two years of fruitful and challenging association with Karl Menninger also has helped to mold my clinical thinking, particularly about a view of psychopathology. Several people have read drafts of the book and have given me the benefit of their cogent criticisms. These include Dr. Gardner Murphy of The Menninger Foundation and Dr. Norman Garmezy of the University of Minnesota, who offered valuable suggestions about content and its presentation. Drs. Harry Trosman and William Offenkrantz of the University of Chicago and the Chicago Psychoanalytic Institute also offered helpful advice. Dr. Linda Hilles of the Mt. Zion Hospital, San Francisco, read the entire manuscript in its several versions and contributed generously to clarifying the text. To her I am particularly appreciative. Hazel Bruce of The Menninger Foundation typed several drafts of the manuscript and in many other ways eased the writing task. Mrs. LaJune Whitney ably typed the final draft and helped with the last details. I am grateful to The Menninger Foundation library staff under the direction of Miss Vesta Walker who helped with the bibliographic compilation. The Hogarth Press has kindly given permission to quote extensively from their *Standard Edition* of Freud's writings. The book was begun when I was on the staff of The Menninger Foundation and was completed after I joined the University of Chicago. I thank both organizations for facilitating my task.

Philip S. Holzman

Contents

CHAPTER 1

INTRODUCTION

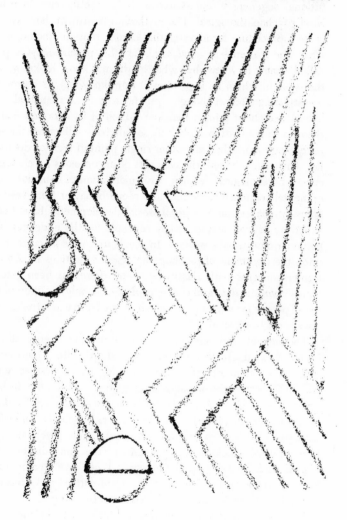

Psychoanalysis is the creation of Sigmund Freud, a Viennese physician whose life spanned about half of the nineteenth century and almost as much of the twentieth century. It began as a method of treatment for some anomalies of behavior which in the past had been labeled "demonic possession" (Sprenger & Kramer, 1948) or congenital or constitutional degeneracy (e.g., Charcot, 1877–1889), but which today we label psychopathological. The method of treatment, however, also became a procedure for investigating human thought, including not only what the patient––or *analysand,* as the psychoanalytic patient is called––knew he knew, but what he did not know he knew, and even the ways in which he kept himself from knowing. As a procedure for investigating human thought, psychoanalysis accumulated a body of knowledge about human behavior. Much of its data and many of the theories worked out to explain those data have influenced the science of psychology more than any other single point of view or discovery thus far. Thus, since Freud, the concepts of unconscious psychological processes, psychological defense, drive-motivation of behavior, and developmental sequences of sexual and social behavior from very early infancy (*psychosexual* and *psychosocial* development) have been established by psychoanalysis as key concepts for the understanding of all behavior, not just the deviant. In psychiatry, with its current emphasis upon the treatment of psychopathological conditions in contrast to its former concerns with classifying them, there has been extensive reliance upon the data and concepts of psychoanalysis although the number of people for whom psychoanalysis is effective as a treatment is, and always has been, small.

The impact of psychoanalysis on culture has been profound. In a humorous vein, Heywood Broun wrote shortly after Freud's death, "At the very moment Freud's ashes are being laid to rest, somewhere an American prize fight manager, sixth-grade class of '98, will be saying, 'the trouble with my heavyweight is the kid's inhibited. He don't know his own strength [1939].' " In the theater, Eugene O'Neill's *Mourning Becomes Electra* owes its spirit and inspiration to psychoanalytic ideas; James Joyce's kaleidoscopic pageants of the mind during the day in *Ulysses* and during sleep in *Finnegans Wake* owe a comparable debt. For since 1900, when Freud's *The Interpretation of Dreams* appeared, the culture of the Western world has never been the same.

The great impact of Freud's ideas is testimony to their scope and brilliance. Yet scientists today are still divided over their validity and their cogency. That these ideas, so many years after their promulgation, remain a matter of bitter controversy deserves some explanation. The explanation may be sought in four places: the nature of the theory, the nature of the method, the training of social scientists, and the training of psychoanalysts.

The Nature of the Theory

What has been called psychoanalytic theory is actually many theories that are loosely tied together—microtheories linked with each other. They are heterogeneous in content and in level of abstraction, and they appear scattered among Freud's papers in both older and newer versions, more as working, tentative formulations than as a final systematic theory. One such group consists of psychoanalytic theories of thought processes such as memory, perception, attention, consciousness, action, emotion, and concept formation; another group is concerned with psychoanalytic conceptions of development; and still another group is a complex of clinical psychoanalytic theories focused on psychopathology and treatment. While some attain a certain theoretical and stylistic elegance, others are rather poorly stated and exist primarily in a pretheoretical form. Some are models rather than theories; that is, they are analogies, comparisons, or constructions that help one visualize a complex mechanism or structure, rather than precise statements of functional relations between variables. The theories and their evolution are not easy to trace since Freud revised and reworked many of them and even abandoned some of them without leaving a final consistent codification. For example, in his first major psychoanalytic work, *The Interpretation of Dreams,* Freud presented in chapters I to VI his theory that dreams were the continuation of daytime preoccupations, that they were motivated by wishes and counterwishes, and that the hallucinatory, nonlogical mode of thinking typical of dreams is quite different from the thought modes of waking life. In the monumental seventh chapter of *The Interpretation of Dreams,* Freud turned his attention from the exploration of the meaning of dreams to an effort to construct a model of the psychic apparatus which would encompass and explain the phenomenon of dreams. In the course of that effort, he proposed a theory of cognition and of consciousness. Eleven years later in his paper entitled "Formulations on the Two Principles of Mental Functioning" (1911b), and again in 1915 and 1917, when he wrote a series of highly theoretical papers called the *metapsychological papers* (*meta*psychological because they went *beyond* what the then current psychological theories were concerned with), he modified the ideas first expressed in *The Interpretation of Dreams*. But he never bothered to rework systematically his old formulations in the light of his new conceptions. Consider one example. In chapter VII of *The Interpretation of Dreams*, Freud discussed consciousness as a sense organ, an apparatus for receiving, but not storing, percepts as well as certain stimuli from within. However, in his 1926 work, *Inhibitions, Symptoms and Anxiety*, he spoke of consciousness as a quality of ideas. Thus, when one refers to the psychoanalytic conception of consciousness or of attention and perception, it is hard to know to which aspects of psychoanalytic theory and to which particular revision of Freud's thinking one is making reference. Freud never undertook a complete systematization of his theories. Even his boldest job of systematizing, chapter VII of *The Interpretation of Dreams*, was incomplete, for it was constructed from one segment of behavioral data, dreams. He never did construct a theory from the data of neurotic behavior or forge an integration of several theories and models. Indeed, in several papers he mentioned his belief that such systematizing and canonizing attempts were premature because there were not enough data for him to set down even a clinical theory in its final form.

Since psychoanalytic theory is multifarious, loose and unformalized, it follows that, contrary to the opinion of some psychologists and even of some psychoanalysts, one need not accept or reject as a whole the body of psychoanalytic findings, assertions, and theories, but may selectively accept or reject, revise or replace parts of them. Some critics reject psychoanalytic propositions because they appear to be stated in terms different from those of other realms of study such as some learning theories, contemporary information theory, or neurophysiology. Meehl, however, remains unconvinced of the requirement that psychoanalysis must be coordinate with other analyses of behavior. "All that one can legitimately require," Meehl wrote, "is that psychoanalytic concepts ought not to be *incompatible* with well-corroborated theories of the learning process or nervous system function. But the situation in these two fields is itself so controversial that this negative requirement imposes only a very weak limitation upon psychoanalytic theorizing [1966]."

The Nature of the Method

Contemporary American psychology as a whole has come to regard the experimental method as the primary valid scientific technique for approximating truth. Psychoanalysis, although empirical in its methods, is not experimental, and to that extent it is out of step with the American psychological community. Yet only in a restricted view would science be limited in its techniques to those of the experimental method. Manipulation and control of variables are not the only scientific procedures. The controlled observation of phenomena, with provision for refuting either the observations or the statements linking them in lawful relations, claims equal status as a scientific method. Many other scientific disciplines follow procedures other than experimental for approximating the truth. Astronomy and geology, for example, depend heavily on the method of careful observation and of conceptualizing relations among phenomena that are observed to vary. Psychoanalysis which begins with observations of human behavior proceeds from just such an empirical base. The constant revision of models and theories in keeping with new observations demonstrates not a weakness but a strength of the method.

Although empirical, psychoanalysis makes no claims to predict behavior. Rather, like history and embryology, it is postdictive. Given a piece of behavior and its antecedents, it attempts to sift the evidence and order it into a pattern which contains the explanation for the behavior. While this method is no less rational than the deductive-predictive approach, it certainly has its own methodological problems; experimental verification must ultimately be introduced as an arbiter of truth.

But the question remains as to when ultimate experimental validation of psychoanalytic formulations should occur. The author of this book agrees that psychoanalytic formulations should be subjected to experimental or other empirical validation but favors a different timing than that demanded by a strict operational or positivistic approach. To guard against nipping preliminary exploration in the bud, there must be a period in which curiosity and inquiry into the unique and novel is fostered while the results of natural observations are awaited and then formalized. Since we can experiment only on what we have already observed, explanations of phenomena, their reduction to scientific laws, and their submission to the rigors of deduction and statistical quantification, as Martin Scheerer has said (1945), can only follow, but not precede, the uncovering of a phenomenon we seek to understand. Robert Oppenheimer, the eminent physicist and philosopher, warned psychologists that quantification is not always the most strategic and enlightening course for science:

> It is not always clear that by measuring one has found something very much worth measuring . . . [measuring] is not necessarily the best way to advance true understanding of what is going on; and I would make this very strong plea for pluralism with regard to methods that, in the necessarily early stages of sorting out an immensely vast experience, may be fruitful and may be helpful [1956].

It is here that naturalistic methods have a crucial role.

From this vantage point, there seem to be two factors that result in inadequate psychoanalytic research. One is premature rigor. The other is its opposite: a casual indifference to instruments of observation, to quantification, to controls, and to replicability of one's observations.

The Training of Social Scientists

Another factor in the controversy over the validity of psychoanalysis is that many sophisticated investigators have a poor knowledge of psychoanalysis. It would be unthinkable for someone to study the behavior of high-speed particles without a thorough grounding in subatomic physics as well as in the scientific method. Yet many investigators, although well trained in sophisticated methodology, have an inadequate knowledge of psychoanalysis. Many have read only secondary sources for their knowledge of psychoanalysis. Few have read completely and in a scholarly manner even half of the legacy of Sigmund Freud, much of which is referred to in the bibliographic references of this book. Yet there seems to be an expectation that these psychologists, their shallow acquaintance with primary source materials notwithstanding, will be able to make compelling translations of psychoanalytic theories or assertions into research proposals.

The Training of Psychoanalysts

Another aspect of the controversy surrounding psychoanalysis implicates the nature of psychoanalytic training in formal institutes. To become a psychoanalyst recognized by the American Psychoanalytic Association, one must receive training under the aegis of one of a limited number of psychoanalytic training institutes accredited by the Association. With few exceptions, these institutes have accepted only psychiatrists as candidates. The effect of this policy of exclusion has been both to make psychoanalysis more and more service-oriented, and the training institutes more and more like trade schools. Scholarly and open discussion and examination of psychoanalytic ideas have tended to become curtailed as professional inbreeding has increased. The isolation of psychoanalysis is increased by the fact that most psychoanalytic institutes are not attached to universities, where the way of life is to expose one's ideas to the scrutiny of colleagues with divergent views. A further effect of the separation of psychoanalytic institutes from universities has been to isolate nonmedical researchers from the fountain of behavioral data from which most psychoanalytic hypotheses spring—the psychoanalytic situation. It is, therefore, somewhat refereshing to see that in a few quarters, not the least of which is the American Psychoanalytic Association itself and some of its institutes, some of this exclusiveness is slowly being corrected.

The Plan of This Book

There is a vast storehouse of information, observation, and unexploited procedures garnered by psychoanalysis. This book attempts to present material from this storehouse. It makes no claim to completeness. It does, however, strive to introduce the reader to some of the evidence on which psychoanalytic ideas are based. A historical presentation will be adopted rather than a premature systematic presentation. This presentation focuses on the first psychopathological phenomena Freud dealt with, his original assertions about them, and their subsequent modification in the light of new psychopathological observations.

From Psychopathology to General Psychology

The survey will highlight an unexpected development in the history of psychoanalysis: Although psychoanalytic theory began as an explanation of abnormal behavior, it reached increasingly into realms of normal functioning until today it seeks to become a general psychology, rather than remain a special theory of psychopathology. This curious turn in the growth of the theory can be traced to the failure of Freud's first theory—in 1894 and 1896—to explain neurotic behavior satisfactorily. We will discuss these early psychoanalytic formulations in Chapter 3. At the time Freud was questioning his first explanations of psychopathology, he was turning his attention inward onto himself. He began to examine his own dreams, fantasies, slips of the tongue, and everyday thoughts. In short, he began to psychoanalyze himself. The data from that endeavor enabled him to reformulate his ideas and to give them more explanatory power than his earlier formulations of 1894 to 1896. But oddly enough, their increased efficiency for explaining psychopathology also vastly broadened the realm of behaviors encompassed by them. Psychoanalysis began to claim as its area of concern not only neurotic symptoms but also nonpathological behaviors such as dreams and slips of the tongue. Still later it included a theory of normal child development, conceptions of sexual and aggressive development, normal or expected conflicts, and the role of the social matrix in which the child grows. These changes in the theory will be traced in Chapters 6 to 9.

Of course, the roots of psychoanalysis remained in psychopathological phenomena. But as the theory grew, Freud became less concerned with delineating precise theories of each form of psychopathological behavior. Thus, although Freud's early work contains a theory of hysteria, of obsessional neurosis, and of paranoia, his later works contain no extended expositions of his changed views of those syndromes. Freud, instead, discussed general concepts of drives, defenses, and other restraining structures and gave brief indications of how these interact in certain psychopathological syndromes. Such a presentation underscores Freud's conviction that diagnostic terms such as hysteria and obsessional neurosis are only names given to extreme variations of personality functioning along certain behavioral dimensions. Thus, there is a continuum between normal and abnormal. Diagnoses in themselves are not real entities, but the behavioral variations which are grouped and named by the diagnoses do have a reality. Anxiety, depression, drive motivation, and styles of defense against inner and outer dangers vary along their own continua. The patterning of extreme forms of behaviors on these continua comprises the psychopathological syndromes. This point of view of psychopathology is a radical departure from the theory of discontinuity of the normal and abnormal that existed at the time Freud began his work. It is important for understanding the Freudian era to examine in the chapter that follows the intellectual setting in which Freud worked.

Summary

Although psychoanalysis is a method of treatment for some psychopathological conditions, it has contributed to an understanding of hitherto unexplored aspects of human behavior such as unconscious mental processes and the sequential development of motivational structures. It has also greatly influenced Western culture. Psychoanalysis is actually a congeries of theories loosely tied together. The theories were constantly revised by Freud in response to the claims of new clinical data. Although psychoanalysis is not primarily experimental, it is an empirical discipline, a characteristic it shares with such sciences as astronomy and geology. Behavioral scientists are divided over the validity of psychoanalytic assertions. This division may be traced both to the nature of the psychoanalytic method (and perhaps the content of the ideas) and to the training of social scientists and of psychoanalysts.

CHAPTER 2

THE INTELLECTUAL BACKGROUND OF PSYCHOANALYSIS: THE CHANGING INTELLECTUAL CURRENTS

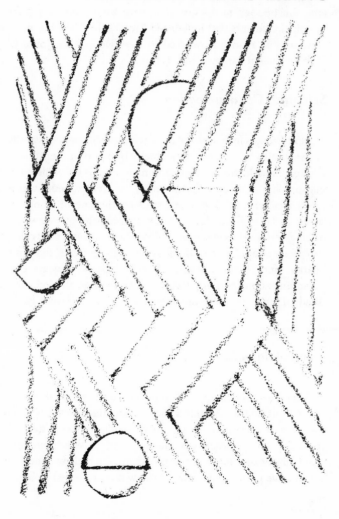

The intellectual background of new ideas both directs them and limits their scope. Therefore, in order to understand the choice of concepts and the focus and impact of a theory, the student should have a realization of the intellectual climate within which the theory was conceived and shaped. This is certainly true for understanding psychoanalysis which is, above all, a theory of man's behavior.

Before one can appreciate the ideas of psychoanalysis, then, some aspects of the intellectual climate of the nineteenth century must be understood. The complete exposition of this aspect of the history of science must be left to the historian; here we present only a sketch of the principal elements that influenced Freud's thinking. For more complete accounts the reader is referred to Bernfeld (1944), Jones (1953), and Holt's excellent survey (Holt, 1963).

Scientific Communication

During Freud's formative years, scientific information was disseminated in the intellectual community chiefly by word of mouth, and therefore the academic lecture was an extremely important vehicle for spreading information. Principally by means of the lecture, professors in universities shared with colleagues and students their new findings and speculations. The use of scientific journals for publishing one's research or theorizing was a relatively new phenomenon and not yet widespread. *Nature,* for example, one of the first scientific journals, did not begin publication until 1869. Because of the relatively slow pace of scientific communication from one institution to another, the influence of the individual professor and the medium of his academic lecture was increased.

Naturphilosophie

The intellectual climate of Europe, and particularly the *Zeitgeist* or the "current of belief" (Boring, 1963) in scientific circles, was rapidly shifting from preoccupations with large metaphysical systems embodying romantic and philosophical themes—called *Naturphilosophie*—to the strict physicalist interpretation of nature which shunned all traces of speculative philosophy. The former was represented in Goethe's "Essay on Nature" which Freud had heard read before he decided to become a physician, the latter principally by the physiology of Helmholtz in Berlin and of Brücke at the University of Vienna where Freud studied.

In Bernfeld's words, proponents of *Naturphilosophie* viewed the universe as "one vast organism, ultimately consisting of forces, of activities, of creations, of emergences [1944]." The universe was organized in eternal basic conflicts, in polarity, and mind was viewed as only a reflection of or an emanation of this turmoil.

Naturphilosophie can be traced to the German philosopher Friedrich Schelling (1775–1854), who taught that the objective world can be understood not only by empirical observation, but by an intuitive understanding of natural phenomena. Such intuition reveals that nature, in both animate and inanimate forms, possesses a "world soul," a concept that, of course, was theological as well as speculative. These ideas, which penetrated the thinking and outlook of most eighteenth- and early nineteenth-century German intellectuals, were an amalgam of Greek thought (particularly that of Heraclitus and Democritus) and theological speculation. They are also an intellectual predecessor of vitalism,[1] a philosophy taught by philosophers, psychologists, and physiologists, among them Henri Bergson and Hans Driesch. For Freud, who had strong speculative tendencies, *Naturphilosophie* represented an attractive lure against which he had to fight vigorously. Yet *Naturphilosophie* shaped Freud's view of man as an organism constantly in conflict not only with his environment but with other men and with himself, and it also fashioned his unique approach of psychoanalysis to man's behavior—a total purposivism. Issues of *why* man behaved as he did received priority over questions of *how* man accomplished his purposes. Moreover, the romantic *Naturphilosophie* probably influenced Freud's attempts to look for explanations of mental phenomena in psychological, rather than in physical, terms.

Physicalism

The speculative excess of the early nineteenth-century intellectual climate was countered and indeed subdued in scientific circles by the

---

[1] *Vitalism* is the name given to explanations of natural phenomena, including human behavior, that emphasized a "vital force" that controls the form and development of activity of living organisms.

physicalist tradition, a tradition that enjoyed extraordinary popularity in German universities when Freud entered medical school in 1873. Thirty-one years earlier, in 1842, Hermann Helmholtz and Carl Ludwig, together with Emil DuBois Reymond in Berlin and Ernst Brücke in Vienna, took an oath which, better than any other description, summed up their strict mechanistic and fundamentally materialistic views.

> No other forces than the common chemical and physical ones are active within the organism. In those cases which cannot at the time be explained by these forces one has either to find a specific way or form of their action by means of physical mathematic method or to assume new forces equal in dignity to the chemical physical forces inherent in matter, reducible to the force of attraction and repulsion [Bernfeld, 1944].

Freud's Training

Freud's scientific training with Brücke, which was thoroughly permeated with this physicalist tradition, turned his interests from philosophical speculation (which he indulged, incidentally, by attending no fewer than five courses given by the philosopher and psychologist Brentano) to research in comparative neuroanatomy. His early training as a scientist gave him a thorough grounding in empirical observation and bore fruit in several remarkable histological and neurological studies. Freud's broad scientific interests during these early years are revealed by his definitive monograph on aphasia (1891), which is still an extraordinary text, his review of the uses of cocaine (1884), and his embryological and histological studies, for example, of the testes of the eel (1877). This strict scientism controlled Freud's romantic philosophy of life; yet both elements are present in his work. The influence of physicalism is most apparent not only in his empirical studies which include the early neuroanatomical and neurological works but also in his later theoretical explanations of mental mechanisms (the so-called "metapsychology"). The influence of *Naturphilosophie* is present in his conflict-view of behavior, in his purposivistic view of man's behavior, in his frankly fanciful excursions such as "Totem and Taboo" (1913b) and "The Future of an Illusion" (1927), and in his grand attempts at a unitary theory represented in his writings on the death instinct.

We must also mention Freud's brief, but influential, training with Charcot and with Liébeault and Bernheim. From Liébeault and Bernheim he learned their techniques of hypnosis in the treatment of hysteria. From Charcot, who undertook a serious investigation of hysterical symptoms—a perplexing variety of physical complaints without demonstrable organic pathology—he learned that these symptoms were genuine phenomena and could even be produced by hypnosis.

The Concept of Energy and the Theory of Evolution

Two other influences on Freud's thought must be noted: the concept of energy and Darwin's theory of evolution.

THE CONCEPT OF ENERGY

Prior to the clear enunciation of the concept of energy in the nineteenth century, physical scientists were working with the concept of *force*. Force, in physics, refers to anything that tends to change the state of rest or motion of a body. Because it is defined as the cause of the movement of material bodies, it is limited to concrete occurrences. Forces can act upon specific objects, but they cannot be considered in the abstract. The concept of energy, defined as the *capacity* to perform work, possesses a degree of abstraction that permits the conception of transformations of energy into various forms—light into heat, for example. Thus, when the concept of energy came into use, the various branches of the physical sciences—electricity, heat, mechanics, for example—could be seen as related to each other in a manner not possible before. In the nineteenth century much excitement was generated by this conceptual breakthrough, and its effects on Freud can be seen in his early use of the energy concept in his paper "The Neuropsychoses of Defense" (1894) and throughout his discussions of drive energies in what has become known as the "economic point of view" in psychoanalysis. Like most scientists of that era, Freud believed that ultimate explanations must first involve forces and ultimately the energy dynamics that explain the forces. It was as fashionable then for scientists to employ the energy concept as it is today for them to make use of the *cybernetic* idea.

Darwin's theory of evolution had, of course, a radical effect on conceptions in the biological sciences—effects which even today are not fully appreciated. The developmental point of view that the species *man* evolves (phylogenetic evolution) and that individual human beings progressively develop (ontogenetic development), although known in the nineteenth century, had to be taken seriously after Darwin. For Freud, assumptions about developmental sequences from infancy through maturity assumed importance, specifically his conception that behaviors or structures in adulthood have their own developmental precursors (an ontogenesis) which can be identified and that such earlier forms of behaviors or structures affect later forms. The Darwinian influence can be seen in Freud's ideas of the development of infantile forms of sexuality into mature adult sexuality or of their failure to develop, as exemplified by disordered or "perverse" behavior. The epigenetic view of sexuality (the idea that sexuality in its mature genital form does not appear suddenly *de novo* but emerges from an orderly developmental sequence which begins in infancy) was perhaps as revolutionary as Darwin's idea of the phylogenetic descent of man and the origin of species. Indeed, this revolutionary view of sexuality was directly derived from Darwinian thought. Darwin's influence can also be discerned in Freud's concepts of adaptive and defensive ego structures. Darwin had called attention to the presence in species of structures that seemed to fit in with specific environments, such as particular ranges of temperature or availability of certain foods. Since these structures presumably ensured the survival of those species in which they were preserved, they represented an advantageous conformation of the organism to the environment. The concept of such adaptive or defensive structures was used by Freud in his theory of defense mechanisms and of adaptive structures (see Chapter 9).

Nineteenth-century Neurology and Psychiatry

In nineteenth-century scientific circles, the nervous system was regarded as a passive structure, with the primary function of ridding itself of externally imposed stimulation. According to the neuroanatomists of that day, the primary function of the billions of nerve fibers found in the human species was to respond to external stimulation by transmitting that stimulation to other fibers or structures, thereby disposing of it. The endogenous rhythms and firings of billions of neuronal cells (the apparent self-stimulations of the central nervous system) which can be visualized on the electroencephalograph and which are taken for granted by twentieth-century physiologists had not yet been discovered.

No theorist should be blamed for what he does not know or for what is not yet known. From the vantage point of mid-twentieth-century neurophysiology, views of the nervous system prior to the theories of Sir Charles Sherrington are unquestionably outmoded. But they were the neurophysiology which Freud had learned and which influenced his theories of organismic action. These nineteenth-century views of nervous activity are reflected at several points in Freud's conceptions. For example, the concept of the *pleasure principle* describes the regulation of organismic tensions by immediate discharge of imposed stimulation. The special theories of drive discharge which will be described in Chapter 8 were also entirely consistent with then modern views of the central nervous system.

The nature of psychiatric practice in the nineteenth century reflected strongly the physicalist reaction against the romantic *Naturphilosophie*. Emotion, faith, and mysticism were eschewed in favor of precise descriptions of disease processes in physical, not psychological, terms. The medical sciences were beginning to experience a noteworthy spurt of growth as a result of several monumental events, such as the statement of the germ theory by Pasteur and the introduction of antiseptic techniques by Lister. The cause of hitherto mysterious ailments was revealed to be physical lesions, as seen in meticulous descriptions of syndromes. The authors of such descriptions include Thomas Addison, who described a disease of the adrenal gland, and Richard Bright, who described a kidney disease. The discovery of the anatomical or organic basis of many illnesses spurred a search by physicians for similar bases for behavior disorders. Theodor Meynert, one of Freud's teachers, believed that inadequate blood circulation was responsible for mental disorders. The German physician Wilhelm Griesinger in 1867 published a textbook of psychiatry which was modeled after texts on medical pathology. Griesinger believed strongly that specific brain lesions could account for all psychopathology. Griesinger wrote:

> The first step towards the knowledge of the symptoms [of insanity] is their locality: to which organ do the indications belong: what organs must necessarily and invariably be diseased where there is madness? . . . Physiological and pathological facts show us that this organ can only be the brain; we, therefore, primarily and in every case of mental disease, recognize a morbid action of that organ [1867].

Nineteenth-century psychiatry was completely organic in its viewpoint. Therapy of the psychopathological disorders, too, depended upon the use of physical means such as baths and sedative drugs. Mild electric currents applied to the muscles of disturbed patients were also employed as in the treatment espoused by Wilhelm Erb in the latter part of the nineteenth century. In the United States just after the Civil War, Silas Weir Mitchell introduced a form of treatment widely used by neurologists and psychiatrists which consisted of rest, much sleep, good but not rich food, and removal from cares and worries.

These, then, were some of the main lines of influence which helped to shape the psychoanalytic view of human behavior.

The theories of Freud represented a sharp break from this materialist tradition in general medicine and in psychiatry in particular. Freud developed a set of explanations that focused not on physical and chemical factors as causative agents but on the life experience of the individual. In this endeavor he merged his physicalist training—with its emphasis on careful observation and logical reasoning—with an appreciation for the fact that psychological activities must, at the present state of knowledge, be considered in psychological, and not in physical, terms. It is curious, however, that Freud always harbored the faith that eventually chemical and neuronal explanations would replace his psychological explanations.

Summary

The intellectual climate in which Freud received his scientific training included the contrasting views of speculative and romantic *Naturphilosophie* and the strict mechanistic and materialistic *physicalism*. Other influences on Freud's intellectual development included the then revolutionary concepts of energy and evolution and nineteenth-century neurology and psychiatry. Nineteenth-century neurology regarded the nervous system as essentially a passive structure; the psychiatry of that time emphasized classificatory efforts and searches for physical causes of psychopathological symptoms.

CHAPTER 3

THE FIRST
PSYCHOPATHOLOGICAL DATA AND
THE EARLIEST ASSUMPTIONS

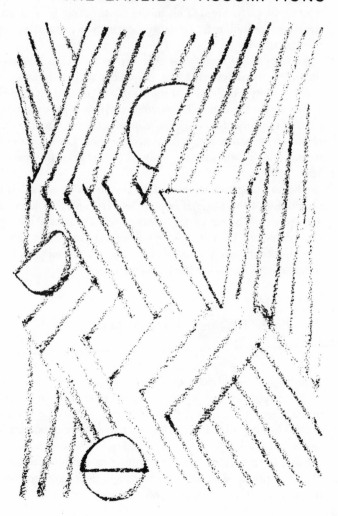

Freud's first formulations on behavior dealt with four groups of neurotic phenomena: hysterical, obsessional, phobic, and paranoid symptoms. Scattered through several of his early papers are vivid descriptions of these four psychopathological conditions existing in patients who presented themselves to him for his help. Had he practiced in a mental hospital, he, no doubt, would have been confronted with different pathological symptoms—those of a more psychotic cast. Freud's subsequent explanations would, thus, have had different emphases, at least in the early stages of his theory construction, for explanatory constructions are built to fit the data produced by a particular sample of the population.

At first most of Freud's patients were middle-class Viennese who reflected the value system, ideals, prejudices, and inhibitions of their section of society. As the size of the sample of patients he treated became larger, and as the national, economic, social, and educational characteristics of the patients became more heterogeneous, Freud's explanations of neurotic behavior required constant revision. Later, children began to come under psychoanalytic study as did adults with character problems.

The widening inclusiveness of the sample makes one's data more representative of the range of human behavior and thus forces a revision and reordering of explanatory conceptions. Theoretical conceptions are expendable, for the basis of the scientific endeavor is reliable observation. Concepts and explanations are merely attempts to systematize, order, and hold together these observations.

The Four "Defense Neuropsychoses"

Before examining the specific attempts Freud made to explain neurotic suffering, we should describe four groups of symptoms—hysterical, obsessional, phobic, and paranoid—that Freud tried to explain. Freud called them the *neuropsychoses of defense* (1894) for reasons we will explore in Chapter 4. Freud's literary talents were considerable and imparted to his acute powers of observation a vividness and lucidity rarely equaled in scientific writing. His writing earned him the Goethe prize. His descriptions of disturbed persons and their psychopathology were noteworthy for their precision and economy.

In describing hysterical patients, for example, he writes of forty-year-old Frau Emmy von N.:

> She still looked young, had finely cut features, full of character. Her face bore a strained and painful expression, her eyebrows were drawn together and her eyes cast down. . . . She spoke in a low voice as though with difficulty and her speech was from time to time subject to spastic interruptions amounting to a stammer. She kept her fingers, which exhibited a ceaseless agitation resembling athetosis [a brain disorder manifested by continual slow movements, particularly of the arms and legs], tightly clasped together. There were frequent convulsive, tic-like movements of her face and the muscles of her neck . . . every two or three minutes she suddenly broke off, contorted her face into an expression of horror and disgust, stretched out her hand towards me, crooking her fingers, and exclaimed, in a changed voice, charged with anxiety: "Keep still!—don't say anything—don't touch me."
>
> She was probably under the influence of some recurrent hallucination of a horrifying kind and was keeping the intruding material at bay with this formula. These interpolations came to an end with equal suddenness and the patient took up what she had been saying, without pursuing her momentary excitement any further, and without explaining or apologizing for her behavior—probably, therefore, without herself having noticed the interpolation [Breuer & Freud, 1893–1895, pp. 83–84].

Recall that when Freud wrote that description, most psychiatrists were focusing on the organic constitutional basis of symptoms. Notice that Freud attempted instead a *psychological* interpretation of one of Frau Emmy's symptoms, thus departing radically from the contemporary psychiatric tradition. Freud found a psychological significance in Frau Emmy's anxious interpolations of "Keep still!—don't say anything—don't touch me!" She was, he assumed, warding off a terrifying experience. This interpretation of behavior as defensive was later to be elaborated into a basic element of psychoanalytic theory.

Another example of a hysterical patient is a woman who suffered from acute shortness of breath which made her fear that she would suffocate. These attacks were accompanied by a buzzing noise in her head, a feeling of giddiness, and a choked feeling in her throat. On occasion she believed that someone was standing behind her ready to seize her, and she described "an awful face that looks at me in a dreadful way, so that I am frightened [Breuer & Freud, 1893–1895, case 4]."

OBSESSIVE-COMPULSIVE NEUROSIS

Freud gave many descriptions of patients with obsessional symptoms. He described a young girl who would continually reproach herself for crimes which she had read about in the newspapers and which she had not committed. If a murder were reported, she would wonder whether she had done it; yet she was aware that her thoughts were ridiculous. Another young girl dreaded the possibility that she would be incontinent and soil her clothes, a fear that prevented her from being with people. When she was alone this fear was not present. Still another patient felt compelled to count the boards in the floor and the steps on the staircase (Freud, 1895a).

PHOBIAS

The third group of patients with whom Freud concerned himself suffered from phobic symptoms; their probias were either exaggerations of usual minor fears, such as of darkness, death, or snakes or the presence of unusual fears that seriously limit freedom of movement, such as of open or closed spaces, bridges, or even walking.

PARANOIA

Freud classified as "paranoid" the final group of symptoms which his patients manifested and which he attempted to explain. He described a young woman, Frau P., who 6 months after the birth of her son became distrustful and suspicious of her husband's family and her neighbors. Soon she believed that other people were accusing her of unspecified wrongdoings and that everyone had lost respect for her. After a short while, she became convinced that people were watching her as she undressed at night and that people were reading her thoughts. Hallucinations of male and female genitals intruded themselves on her thoughts, particularly when she was in the company of other women (Freud, 1896).

Nineteenth-century Psychiatric Explanations

CHARCOT'S AND JANET'S EXPLANATIONS

For centuries people with such symptoms had come to the attention of society's jailers, witch-hunters, magicians, and physicians. By the middle of the nineteenth century, no one still seriously believed that such persons were possessed by evil spirits, as they had once believed during the sixteenth, seventeenth, and eighteenth centuries. Alternate explanations were sought. Because these patients were unable to explain their symptoms and because some patients, although they seemed quite normal in other ways, were apparently quite unaware of their own symptoms, nineteenth-century authorities such as Charcot and Janet maintained that these conditions were indications of a second state of consciousness. They referred to it as a *splitting of consciousness* which permitted the symptomatic behavior to enjoy a separate existence from the patient's large areas of nonsymptomatic behavior. Both these physicians attempted to explain the cause of splitting. Charcot's explanation (1877–1889) emphasized the hereditary disposition of the patient. Charcot's pupil Janet was on the verge of developing a psychological theory of hysteria. He recognized the importance of nonconscious factors—he called them *automatisms*—but he fully believed that the existence of psychopathological symptoms was evidence of the "hereditary degeneracy [Janet, 1884]." The theories of Charcot and Janet were principally somatic and failed to explain how particular symptoms arose in particular people.

JOSEF BREUER'S EXPLANATION

Josef Breuer, Freud's teacher and later his collaborator on the "Studies on Hysteria" (Breuer & Freud, 1893–1895), also formulated a theory to account for splitting. Breuer, a scientist and physician in the physicalist tradition, had done outstanding research both on the physiology of respiration (under Ewald Hering), and on the role of the semicircular canals in maintaining balance and posture. He shunned an academic career, however, and entered private practice in 1871, although he continued his close association with the proponents of strict scientism such as Brücke, Exner, Hering, and Mach.

Breuer based his theory on observations of a single hysterical patient whose symptoms seemed to disappear one by one when she recalled with intense emotion the circumstances of their onset. In 1880 Breuer had undertaken the treatment of a girl in her early twenties. Anna O., as the patient was referred to, seemed to be a veritable household of hysterical symptoms: among them were contractures of her arms and legs, visual disturbances and impairments, and a nervous cough. She would occasionally lapse into a trancelike state during which she apparently experienced hallucinations and sometimes mumbled a few words. One day, while in this peculiar trance state, she told Breuer about some of her symptoms, and to his astonishment the symptoms then disappeared. The patient herself realized the value of this occurrence, and she continued her "talking cure," as she called it. This procedure, undertaken daily in the presence of Breuer, resulted in great, if temporary, improvement. Breuer then discovered that if he induced a hypnotic trance and instructed Anna O. to recall situations surrounding the onset of particular symptoms, those symptoms would disappear, apparently permanently, provided the recollections were accompanied by intense emotion. The experience seemed quite consistent: the recall, with affect, of the circumstances which had precipitated these symptoms resulted in their disappearance. Breuer called the process by which the patient expressed the affect associated with the symptom *abreaction.*

From his treatment experience with Anna O., Breuer explained the splitting which occurs in hysteria by assuming the occurrence of altered states of consciousness which he called *hypnoid states.* Such states, he argued, tend to develop spontaneously under special circumstances, for example, as in the "broodings of a care-ridden man, the anxiety of a person watching at the sick bed of someone dear to him, the daydreams of a lover," or during intense absorption of interest in a problem. According to Breuer, the ideas which arise during hypnoid states are blocked from easy commerce and communication with the contents of "normal consciousness." Thus, wrote Breuer:

> We find, under hypnosis, among the causes of hysterical symptoms ideas which are not in themselves significant, but whose persistence is due to the fact that they originated during the prevalence of severely paralyzing affects, such as fright, or during positively abnormal psychic states, such as

the semihypnotic twilight state of daydreaming, autohypnoses, etc. In such cases it is the nature of the states which makes a reaction to the event impossible . . . since in autohypnosis criticism and supervision by reference to other ideas is diminished and, as a rule, it disappears almost completely, the wildest delusions may arise from it and remain untouched for long periods. Thus it is almost only in these states that there arises a somewhat complicated irrational "symbolic relation between the precipitating cause and the pathological phenomenon" which indeed is often based on the most absurd similarities of sound and verbal associations [Breuer & Freud, 1893–1895, p. 45].

Breuer presumed that another cause of hysteria lay in circumstances which prevented appropriate motor and affective response to an exciting or traumatic situation. The excitement was "retained," presumably in the memory trace of the exciting event, awaiting only the proper releasing circumstances. He called this condition *retention hysteria*.

Although Breuer's theory was a more psychological one than those of Charcot and Janet, neither hypnoid nor retention hysteria was conceived of in terms of a conflict or in terms of forces preventing the emergence of ideas into consciousness. The cause was thus purely adventitious. Although these constructs of causation seemed to fit those few cases where the patient easily verbalized precipitating factors—as, for example, Anna O. did—they did not explain the majority of cases. Indeed, for most patients, therapeutically induced abreactions had no ameliorative effect, and hypnosis did not at all facilitate recall. Freud tried to theorize about the symptoms of the large majority of patients, not just the few; for him the nonmotivational explanations offered by the French and by Breuer were not adequate.

Freud's First Theory: Defensive Behavior

At first Freud adopted Breuer's therapeutic method: he talked with his patients, and he listened to them for long periods, an hour a day for several days a week, often for several weeks. In talking with his patients and in trying to facilitate their recall of the supposedly causal traumatic events, Freud, like Breuer, was impressed by what he heard. His patients told him, with some difficulty, that they had had pervasively unpleasant experiences which were incompatible with their conceptions of themselves and with their sense of morality or with their sense of pride. These experiences invariably were sexual seductions that had occurred shortly before the hysterical episode. Because the experiences were intensely disturbing, the patients had tried to forget them. But the events were more than unpleasant. They were also highly exciting, and the patients found forgetting them difficult. Freud speculated that other people who had comparable experiences were able to forget them completely and, therefore, did not fall ill. But for Freud's patients, however, the task of forgetting could not be achieved. It seemed to Freud that his patients tried to deal with the memories—that is, to defend themselves against them—by *diminishing* the attached affect, so that ideas once strong in character became weak and could then be virtually obliterated. The techniques—Freud termed them *defenses*—that the patient used to deal with the pathogenic ideas will be discussed in Chapter 4. Here we only wish to indicate that these defensive techniques differed in hysteria, phobias, obsessional disorders, and paranoia.

THE ISSUE OF DETERMINISM

The first general assumption that Freud made about neurotic symptoms was that they were caused: that they had specific determinants or antecedent conditions which could be discovered. In this respect he was following the physicalistic tradition of Helmholtz. This assumption of *determinism* permeates the entire Freudian literature as a fundamental assumption and is the foundation of all the later insights of psychoanalysis. Freud further realized that knowledge of necessary conditions of an event does not always give a complete explanation of the cause.[1] Particularly in human behavior, which is so complex, it is rarely possible to find single causes that are both necessary and sufficient, as was so dramatically shown by the Pasteur and Koch experiments on bacterial infections. Indeed, in human behavior what appears as a sufficient cause at one time may not be so at another time. That one must search for

---

[1] *Necessary conditions* are those that must be present for an event to take place. If a man has a diagnosed case of pulmonary tuberculosis, one necessary condition for the disease to have developed is the presence in the body of the tubercle bacillus. But the mere presence of the tubercle bacillus is not a complete or sufficient explanation of the cause of the disease, for there are many people in whom tubercle bacilli are found who do not have clinical tuberculosis.

many apparently sufficient causes as explanations of behavior—and Freud considered neurotic symptoms as classes of behavior—became for Freud a fundamental principle which he called the *principle of overdetermination*. It is quite apparent that Freud, like the British philosopher Hume, was aware that the assumption of determinism was indeed only an assumption and a belief, but that it was an assumption which made scientific inquiry possible.

The principle of strict determinism in Freud's theory does not involve identifying precisely the necessary and sufficient mechanical causes of behavior. It does involve specifying the psychological *motivations* for behavior. From the point of view of the suffering patient, symptoms are psychologically motivated in the sense that they serve purposes. Furthermore, Freud assumed that it is possible to discover from the history of the symptoms the causal motives or purposes that underlay the symptoms. The converse, however, is not true; a knowledge of purpose and motive does not always permit predictable behavioral outcomes. Thus Freud's idea that symptoms reflect defensive behaviors was an unequivocal assumption that neurotic symptoms were motivated. Constitutional explanations had ignored the question of psychological causation, and the hypnoidal theory equally had ignored the question of specific causality, for it held that a traumatic experience was an inadvertent chance event that merely "happened" while the patient was in a hypnoid state.

UNCONSCIOUS PSYCHOLOGICAL PROCESSES

Freud's second major assumption about symptoms implicated *unconscious psychological processes*. He assumed that ideas are to be considered as mental phenomena even though they may not be conscious at any particular moment. The evidence for unconscious psychological processes came to Freud from various sources. One of these was from his studies of hypnotic phenomena under Charcot at Paris and under Bernheim and Liébeault at Nancy. He became particularly impressed by the phenomenon of posthypnotic suggestion which forced upon him the conclusion that past experiences could survive outside of awareness as latent memories, that these could be activated by a signal and could then influence behavior, while the hypnotized person was unaware of the reasons for his behavior. Freud was also impressed that under hypnosis his patients could recall unpleasant or highly arousing experiences which, although not readily recalled in the waking state, nevertheless seemed to be preserved with a startling freshness. The nature of such unconscious psychological processes will be considered in greater detail in Chapter 5.

Keep in mind the two assumptions of psychological determinism and unconscious psychological processes as we turn now to the specific explanations advanced by Freud to account for hysterical, obsessional, phobic, and paranoid symptoms.

Summary

Freud's earliest theories about psychopathological behavior were based on his interviews with middle-class Viennese patients. Under the rubric "the neuropsychoses of defense," he classified patients with hysterical, obsessive-compulsive, phobic, and paranoid symptoms. Because these patients were often unable to account for their symptoms, several psychiatrists, like Charcot and Janet, explained the pathological symptoms by the concept of "splitting of consciousness," which implied a hereditary disposition to develop such a state. Breuer, however, attributed the cause of splitting to the existence of hypnoid states during which appropriate reactions to dramatic events were prevented. Freud's explanation emphasized the psychological meaning of the symptoms and the purposes they served in a patient's life. His explanations rested on two assumptions: (1) all behavior is purposeful and indeed several purposes frequently underlie a particular symptom; and (2) consciousness is not an invariant accompaniment of mental processes.

CHAPTER 4

THE FIRST EXPLANATIONS
OF PSYCHOPATHOLOGICAL STATES

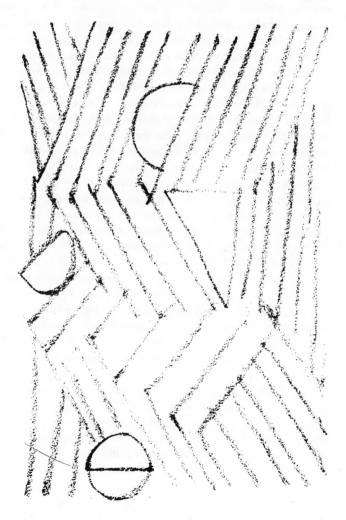

Hysterical Symptoms: The Concept of "Splitting"

In reviewing the contemporary theories of hysteria, Freud (1894) focused on the formulations of Janet and Breuer. Both men had assumed that hysteria reflected two states of mind which were separated or dissociated from each other. They drew their conclusions from clinical interviews of hysterical patients who, when asked to talk about their illness, showed an astonishing lack of awareness of how and even when their symptoms developed. Often the more insistent the doctor's questioning became, the vaguer became the patients' explanations. Furthermore, many patients seemed quite indifferent to the enormous inconvenience which the symptoms caused them. It was as if the hysterical symptoms and the ideas associated with them were cut off—"split"—from the rest of the contents of consciousness. Thus in the theories of Janet and Breuer, "splitting" was the concept that explained hysteria. Actually, *splitting* is simply a name given to the observation that patients seemed cut off from their symptoms.

But "splitting" itself required an explanation. For Janet and Charcot, as discussed in Chapter 3, the explanation was an innate weakness of the patient. For Breuer, it was the presence of hypnoidal states. Both explanations lacked the factor of psychological motivation which Freud considered to be a necessary ingredient in a theory of the development of a hysterical attack. For Freud, a good theory had to include a statement of causation. Simply naming a phenomenon did not suffice; nor did he accept an explanation that bypassed psychological causes, as did concepts of constitutional weakness. Psychological factors were as real to him as physical factors. In the patients Freud saw, there was no question of hereditary weaknesses; indeed, the patients seemed to have enjoyed good health up to a certain time in their lives when something abhorrent to their moral sensitivity occurred. Nor could Freud convince himself that his patients were in an altered state of consciousness when the disagreeable event or events occurred. Freud applied his physicalist training to behavior and assumed that regularities underlie behavior, that the scientist must become aware of these regularities and then inform himself about all the parameters of the behavior in question.

The Role of the Traumatic Experience

THE PSYCHOANALYTIC METHOD

In talking with his patients, Freud thought he had discovered the convincing regularity he searched for. No doubt his therapeutic technique gave him access to these regularities. He had learned from Breuer's treatment of Anna O. that much can be discovered about a patient's inner experiences—even those apparently long forgotten—by allowing the patient to talk freely. At first, following the lead of Bernheim, he tried hypnosis as a method of facilitating a patient's recall, but soon he became dissatisfied with the technique as too demanding and the therapeutic results as too unstable. He then turned to Breuer's *cathartic method* (the method of abreaction) and developed it far beyond Breuer's use of it with Anna O. Freud had the patient lie in a supine position on a couch while he sat behind the couch out of sight of the patient—a remnant of the hypnotic technique. He scheduled treatment interviews for 1 hour each day, 6 days a week. He required the patient to tell him everything that came to mind, regardless of how unimportant, embarrassing, or silly the thoughts may have seemed. When, in his early efforts with this technique, a patient felt blocked and unable to think of any thoughts, Freud would press his hand on the patient's forehead and suggest that ideas would appear. Later he abandoned this "pressure" technique and simply instructed his patients to associate freely.

> Act as though, for instance, you were a traveler sitting next to the window of a railway carriage and describing to someone inside the carriage the changing views which you see outside [Freud, 1913, p. 135].

Even this earliest method revealed to Freud his patients' thoughts, fantasies, and feelings that usual interview questions would have obscured. Thus, he heard from 17 of 17 patients that just preceding the hysterical attack, the patient had experienced an upsetting event which was sexual in nature. Freud saw an additional curious regularity. All patients shared a great difficulty in recalling such events. Although Freud was not convinced that sexual experiences were the *sine qua non* of neurotic conflicts, he was impressed with both the consistency of their occurrence in his patients' experience and the patients' difficulty in recalling them. Freud reasoned that apparently the experiences were so distressing and so antithetical to the patients' moral stance that they tried to forget them, as normal people do. But for Freud's patients the attempt to forget was not successful, and the noxious residue of the experiences led to the pathological formations of hysteria, obsessional neurosis, and hallucinatory psychosis. There was no need to assume a constitutional degeneracy as the principal pathological agent.

A case illustration: Katharina. Here is an illustration, from the "Studies on Hysteria," of the clinical data Freud gathered. He was vacationing in the Alps, and after he had just reached the top of a 6,000-foot mountain, an eighteen-year-old girl startled him by asking him if he were a doctor. She told him that her nerves were bad and that she felt that she would suffocate and die. She reported that in addition to these feelings, she had spells in which she saw an awful face in front of her, a face which she did not recognize. Freud surmised that the girl was describing a typical hysterical attack.

"Do you know what your attacks come from?" [asked Freud].
"No."
"When did you first have them?"
"Two years ago, while I was still living on the other mountain with my aunt. But they keep on happening."
Was I to make an attempt at an analysis? . . . Perhaps I might succeed with a simple talk. I should have to try a lucky guess.
. . . So I said, "If you don't know, I'll tell you how *I* think you got your attacks. At that time, two years ago, you must have seen or heard something that very much embarrassed you, and that you'd much rather not have seen."
"Heavens yes!" she replied, "that was when I caught my uncle with a girl, with Franziska, my cousin."
"What's this story about a girl? Won't you tell me all about it?"
"You can say *anything* to a doctor, I suppose. Well, at that time, you know, my uncle—the husband of the aunt . . . kept the inn. Now they are divorced, and it's my fault they were divorced, because it was through me that it came out that he was carrying on with Franziska."
"And how did you discover it?"
"This way. One day two years ago some gentleman had climbed the mountain and asked for something to eat. My aunt wasn't at home, and Franziska, who always did the cooking, was nowhere to be found. And my

uncle was not to be found either. We looked everywhere, and at last Alois, the little boy, my cousin, said, 'Why, Franziska must be in father's room!' And we both laughed; but we weren't thinking anything bad. Then we went to my uncle's room but found it locked. That seemed strange to me. Then I looked in [the window], the room was rather dark, but I saw my uncle and Franziska; he was lying on her."

"Well?"

"I came away from the window at once, and leaned up against the wall and couldn't get my breath—just what happens to me since. Everything went blank, my eyelids were forced together and there was a hammering and buzzing in my head."

"Why were you so frightened when you found them together? Did you understand it? Did you know what was going on?"

"Oh no. I didn't understand anything at that time. I was only sixteen."

"Fräulein Katharina, if you could remember now what was happening in you at that time, when you had your first attack, what you thought about it—it would help you."

"Yes, if I could. But I was so frightened that I've forgotten everything."

"Tell me, Fräulein. Can it be that the head you always see when you lose your breath is Franziska's head, as you saw it then?"

"Oh no, she didn't look so awful. Besides, it's a man's head."

"Or perhaps your uncle's?"

"I didn't see his face as clearly as that."

She then spoke about how a few days later she felt ill and nauseated. Freud suggested to her that perhaps since she was ill, what she saw might have made her feel disgusted. The girl replied that it was too dark to see anything. She said that she had, however, reported the incident to her aunt and that there had followed some disagreeable scenes which resulted in a separation between her aunt and uncle, particularly because Franziska had become pregnant. Freud continued the story:

After this, however, to my astonishment she dropped these threads and began to tell me two sets of older stories, which went back two or three years earlier than the traumatic moment. The first set related to occasions on which the same uncle had made sexual advances to her herself, when she was only fourteen years old. She woke up suddenly "feeling his body" in the bed. When I asked her if she knew what he was trying to do to her, she replied, "Not at the time." It had become clear to her much later on, she said; she had resisted because it was unpleasant to be disturbed in one's sleep and "because it wasn't nice." . . . She went on to tell me of yet other experiences of a somewhat later date: how she had once again had to defend herself against him in an inn when he was completely drunk, and similar stories. Once the whole family had spent the night in their clothes in a hayloft and she was woken up suddenly by a noise; she thought she noticed that her uncle, who had been lying between her and Franziska, was turning away, and that Franziska was just lying down.

At the end of these two sets of memories she came to a stop. She was like someone transformed. The sulky, unhappy face had grown lively, her eyes were bright, she was lightened and exalted. Meanwhile the understanding of her case had become clear to me. The later part of what she had told me, in an apparently aimless fashion, provided an admirable explanation of her behavior at the scene of the discovery. At that time she had carried about with her two sets of experiences which she remembered but did not understand, and from which she drew no inferences. When she caught sight of the couple in intercourse, she at once established a connection between the new impression and these two sets of recollections, she began to understand them and at the same time to fend them off. There then followed a short period of working out, of "incubation", after which the symptoms of conversion set in, the vomiting as a substitute for moral and physical disgust. This solved the riddle. She had not been disgusted by the sight of the two people but by the memory which that sight had stirred up in her. And, taking everything into account, this could only be the memory of the attempt on her at night when she had "felt her uncle's body."

So when she had finished her confession I said to her, "I know now what it was that you thought when you looked into the room. You thought: 'Now he is doing with her what he wanted to do with me that night and those other times.' That was what you were disgusted at, because you remembered the feeling when you woke up in the night and felt his body."

"It may well be," she replied, "that that was what I was disgusted at and that that was what I thought."

What about the recurrent hallucination of the head, which appeared during her attacks and struck terror into her? Where did it come from? I proceeded to ask her about it, and, as though *her* knowledge, too, had been extended by our conversation, she promptly replied, "Yes, I know now. The head is my uncle's head—I recognize it now—but not from *that* time. Later, when all the disputes had broken out, my uncle gave way to a senseless rage against me. He kept saying that it was all my fault: if I hadn't chattered, it would never have come to a divorce. He kept threatening he would do something to me; and if he caught sight of me at a distance his face would get distorted with rage and he would make for me with his hand raised. . . ."

I hope this girl, whose sexual sensibility had been injured at such an early age, derived some benefit from our conversation. I have not seen her since [Freud, 1895, case 4].

The Clinical Inferences: Defensive Behavior

Neurotic patients, in Freud's view, were thus behaving purposefully. The nature of the purposes—the theory of motivation—went through many changes in Freud's thinking, but it is quite clearly stated at each phase of his theory-building. In this first early period, in the middle 1890s, he considered that the purpose of certain neurotic symptoms was to reject from consciousness something that was unpleasant to a part of oneself. This purpose existed, he believed, in the symptoms of the syndromes which he called *defense neuropsychoses:* hysteria, obsessional neurosis, phobias, and hallucinatory psychosis (1894), although not in those of a number of other psychopathological conditions which he referred to as *actual neuroses,* such as anxiety neurosis, hypochondriasis, and neurasthenia. For the patients suffering from defense neuropsychoses, the idea to be warded off was the memory of an exciting event. But because of the great excitement attached to it, the idea was difficult to eradicate from memory. Anything which could diminish the excitement would decrease the painfully insistent capacity of the idea to remind the person of the shameful experience. From his patients Freud learned the ways or mechanisms by which people maneuvered to obliterate, mollify, or mitigate the excitement or the affective component of the memory. Freud called these ways of fending off *defenses* and conceived of them as mechanisms leading to symptom formation. Although the hysterical, obsessional, and hallucinatory patients all tried to forget the disagreeable events by dealing with the affective component, each group of patients used different and specific defensive maneuvers. Put another way, Freud introduced a concept of defense to explain the fact that his patients could not tell him about or even easily remember the crucial offensive events; thus, Freud invoked the concept of defense to explain the phenomenon of "splitting" of consciousness. The different defenses which Freud discovered to be in operation in each of the "neuropsychoses of defense" deserve review.

DEFENSES IN HYSTERIA

In hysteria, the patient attempted to control a painful memory by weakening it through a withdrawal of the affect associated with it. The affect thus separated from the memory-idea became transformed into some bodily innervation by a process Freud called *conversion.* It was this affect in the form of the bodily symptom which, then, as the symbol of the noxious memory, became the burden for the patient. The idea of the memory, however, remained in its weakened state outside awarness. Only at such a time as it linked itself with new experiences and their associated affects could the memory return to consciousness. Thus the weakened memories could not be voluntarily recalled; they could, however, be recognized if proper new experiences occurred. Such recognition could again trigger the original pain associated with the earlier memory, and a new effort at defense would then be required.

The steps, then, in this hypothetical process were (1) a traumatic experience that is incompatible with the patient's moral sense; (2) the patient's attempt to eradicate the memory of that event by weakening the idea through draining off its associated affect; (3) conversion of the affect into somatic channels resulting in somatic symptoms; and (4) the instability of this defense in the light of new, related experiences, resulting in a return to consciousness of the memory of the traumatic experience.

Freud was well aware that in this explanation he had to assume the existence of a hypothetical energy. In his words:

> I should like finally to dwell for a moment on the working hypothesis which I have made use of in the exposition of the neuroses of defense. I refer to the concept that in mental functions something is to be distinguished which possesses all the attributes of a quantity (though we have no means of measuring it) which is capable of increase, diminution, displacement and discharge, and which is spread over the memory-traces of ideas, somewhat as an electric charge is spread over the surface of a body.
>
> This hypothesis . . . can be applied in the same sense as physicists apply the hypothesis of a flow of electric fluid. It is provisionally justified by its utility in coordinating and explaining a great variety of psychical states [1894, pp. 61–62].

According to Freud, the choice of this complex of defensive processes that led to hysteria was to be sought in the patient's disposition—*possibly constitutional in origin*—for dealing with large quantitites of excitement by converting them into somatic innervation. Disposition in this context refers not to the patient's propensity to become ill, but to the form his illness will take *if* he should become ill. The manifestation of his illness will be guided by the dispositions inherent in his character structure as a template guides or molds a form. Thus at this early stage in the development of his theory of psychopathology, Freud formulated a scheme that still has great cogency: the patient's character pertains to his style of adaptation which antedates the development of symptoms. Although character is independent of illness, it implies certain vulnerabilities as well as strengths and sets a pattern for both growth and illness.

In 1896, after he had accumulated about 2 more years of clinical experience, Freud asked himself why these traumatic events resulted in hysterical symptoms in some people and not in others. A predisposition to the defense of conversion was not sufficient to explain the condition. As he listened to his patients' free associations, he heard reports of still earlier traumatic events—all involving recollections of the stimulation of their genital organs by another person—which had occurred even before puberty, indeed even as early as the age of seven or eight. These events, Freud reasoned, primed the patients for the impact of the later trauma, although at the time of their occurrence, they did not alarm the patient. Only with the onset of the later sexual experiences were the earlier occasions of passive sexual seductions revivified. Freud thus postulated a biphasic disease process: (1) an early sexual event, such as a seduction, which conditioned the child for the impact of a later sexual event and (2) a later sexual event which acted as a stressor to release the disease process. Neither the first nor the second condition *alone* was sufficient for the occurrence of hysterical symptoms. It is important to note that in most of Freud's cases the identity of the seducer was alleged to be the parent of the patient. Consequently the childhood sexual seductions were specially abhorrent because they involved incestuous experiences. Thus, in a footnote to the case study of Katharina, added 31 years after its publication, Freud wrote:

> I venture after the lapse of so many years to lift the veil of discretion and reveal the fact that Katharina was not the niece but the daughter of the landlady. The girl fell ill, therefore, as a result of sexual attempts on the part of her own father [Breuer & Freud, 1893–1895, p. 134].

DEFENSES IN OBSESSIVE-COMPULSIVE NEUROSIS

The term "obsessive-compulsive neurosis" refers to people who experience persistent unwelcome, inconsequential, or frightening ideas or recurrent, irresistible urges to perform certain acts. The acts have a ritual quality, and they may include repetitive unnecessary hand-washing or repetitive touching of certain objects. The personality characteristics of people who manifested these symptoms included perfectionism, circumstantiality, indecisiveness, a moralistic stance, a rather stiff and formal demeanor, and an appearance of being cold and without emotion. These people, clearly, were characterologically different from the hysterical neurotics who, in contrast, appeared as emotionally labile, impulsive, naïve, and who retreated from ideational activities. Thus not only the symptoms, but also the character structures of the two classes of neurotics differed, and Freud had to take these differences into account in describing the way in which the obsessive-compulsive neurotic defended himself against a childhood sexual experience.

Freud maintained that there were people who, because they did not have the capacity for conversion of affect, had to defend themselves in a different fashion. For some of these people, after the separation of the affect from the memory, the affect remained as a psychological rather than a somatic factor but became attached to other ideas which were not incompatible with the person's representation of himself. Thus, for example, an animal like a horse might be feared instead of the person who attempted to seduce the patient. These previously trivial ideas became endowed with an intensity not warranted by their reality reference, while the originally offending ideas remained weakened. Freud referred to this mechanism of defense as *displacement* or *transposition*. The ideas upon which the affect was displaced then had an insistence that could be bothersome. In some instances they appeared as phobic fears, in others as obsessional ideas or preoccupations. In contrast to their fate in hysteria, in obsessive-compulsive conditions the originally unwelcome ideas remained conscious or easily available to consciousness but lacked intensity.

Within two years time, Freud became dissatisfied with his explanation of obsessive-compulsive neurosis, just as he had with that of hysteria, and turned his attention to the alleged experiential factors responsible for obsessional forms of symptoms. From his patients' free associations he had discovered that in hysteria, memories of passively experienced sexual seductions were distasteful to the patient and needed expunging from awareness. In obsessive-compulsive neuroses, he surmised that sexual experiences had occurred in which the patient had been an active seducer, although these had been preceded by sexual encounters passively experienced by the patient. Freud thought of the obsessional ideas as transformed self-reproaches for the forgotten childhood immoralities. He regarded the development of obsessional neurosis as a four-stage process. During the *first* phase—occurring perhaps at the age of seven to nine years—a passive seduction occurs, and this is followed by the child actively involving another child in sexual play. Thus a passive experience is turned into an active one. The period closes with the appearance of sexual maturity. The *second* period begins when self-reproaches are attached to the memory of events during the period of childhood immorality. These self-reproaches press the child to take cognitive action to reduce the pain of self-reproaches, and a period of primary defense is ushered in. In this phase the recollections of the active sexual seductions are replaced by efforts at conscientiousness and perfectionism and by feelings of shame and of self-distrust. The *third* period is one of apparent health, during which these defenses—reactions against the early immorality—seem to be successful in reassuring the person of his essential morality. In the *fourth* phase there is a failure of the defense formations and the struggles of phase 2 are renewed.

Whether the failure of the defense processes occurred spontaneously or whether some new sexual excitation triggered it, Freud was not prepared to say. Nevertheless, the self-reproaches returned in a new form expressing new content and represented compromises between the memory of the early sexual experiences and the forces defending against them at the behest of the patient's morality and self-representation. Freud put it rather epigrammatically: "Obsessional ideas are invariably transformed *self-reproaches* which have reemerged from *repression* [1] and which always relate to some sexual act that was performed with pleasure in childhood [1896, p. 169].

DEFENSES IN PARANOIA

Paranoia refers to patients who, while neither manifestly confused nor excessively disturbed in their behavior, nevertheless have well-developed delusions whose content is generally persecutory or religious. The character structure of patients with paranoia emphasizes

[1] The term *repression* has a very special meaning in psychoanalysis. We will discuss its meaning in detail in Chapter 7. Apparently Freud first used the term in 1893 in the introductory chapter to the "Studies on Hysteria" written by Breuer and Freud. In this first usage, "repression" (*Verdrängung*) is used interchangeably with "defense" (*Abwehr*). In later usage, however, Freud designated repression as one specific defense among many.

suspiciousness, overcautiousness, and a legalistic way of thinking. Freud considered paranoia to be another "defense neuropsychosis" and that the defensive process in paranoia represented a third way of warding off the memories of the early traumatic events.

This third defensive process described by Freud had more serious pathological consequences than did those involved in hysterical and obsessional disorders. There were some people who, Freud ascertained, dealt with the memories of traumatic events by denying that the experiences had ever occurred. This *denial* of reality, when carried to some limit, became the condition for a psychotic state; for, insofar as a piece of reality was rejected, the person had loosened himself from the constraints of the real world. According to Freud, this denial of reality was a necessary condition for the development of delusional thinking and even for the creation of hallucinations with a persecutory content. Freud had been able to trace the hallucinations and delusional thoughts of one patient (he had only an occasional psychotic patient to treat) back to allegedly actual childhood experiences. The recollections of the childhood immorality were repressed either by or with the help of a self-reproach as in the obsessional disorders. Then at a later period, after a phase of apparent health, the defense failed—just why it failed Freud did not understand—and the patient experienced a return of self-reproach.

Thus the difference between obsessional neurosis and paranoia seemed to be this: In the obsessional disorders, the patient recognized his self-reproach as in some sense justified, for he was still dimly aware of his earlier transgressions; furthermore, the reproaches resulted in serviceable conscientiousness. In paranoia, on the other hand, the patient not only rejected the memory of the original events and denied the occurrence of the early events, but he also *projected* the reproaches so that he felt them to come from others. This defensive device brought with it suspicion and distrust of others.

Freud's discovery of meaning in neurotic and psychotic symptoms was not novel, for Breuer had already demonstrated it in his patient Anna O. Yet Freud could not explain the choice of specific psychotic symptoms, that is, why in some cases of paranoia the reproaches returned as thoughts spoken aloud—auditory hallucinations—while in other cases they were imagined rebukes from other people. Nor could he fully understand the choice of neurotic symptoms, a problem that is equally puzzling today. The kinds of explanations, however, that Freud began to develop proved to be productive of new discoveries and new ways of looking not only at psychopathology but at normal personality development as well. Freud's emphasis was on *conflict*—a dialectic between traumatic events or the recollection of them and the person's representation of himself. In this dialectic the two antithetical parts of the conflict compromise in a synthesis that preserves both elements of the struggle yet is finally neither one nor the other. Thus, in symptoms there are to be recognized both the defending process and that which is defended against, the representation of the trauma and the attempts to obliterate it. The implications of this point of view and of the many concepts implicit in it will be examined in the next chapter.

Before we end this exposition of Freud's earliest explanations of some neurotic conditions—the explanations were limited only to the defense neuropsychoses and were not generalized to all of psychopathology—we must anticipate what is to follow. Freud soon discovered a basic error in his formulations, an error that forced him to rethink his entire theory. He discovered that his patients had not necessarily *experienced* in reality the sexual events that they related. Indeed many of his patients had been telling him their *fantasies* about their childhood rather than their actual experiences. Once this transposition became clear to Freud, he began to develop astounding insights into those personal psychological experiences that mold personality and that can lead one to competence or to pathology.

Summary

The concept of "splitting," employed principally by Charcot and Janet, failed to explain how and why neurotic symptoms developed. Using the data of his patients' "free associations," Freud formulated the hypothesis that in the neuropsychoses of defense, conflict was a principal variable. In particular, Freud assumed that all patients were trying to defend themselves against the memories of experiences—generally sexual—that were incompatible with their moral attitudes toward themselves. Four types of symptoms—hysterical, obsessional, phobic, and paranoid—represented the outcome of different kinds of defenses against the memory of the traumaic sexual event. The type of defense adopted by the patient reflected, in part, constitutional dispositions to deal with the sexual conflicts in particular ways and, in part, the nature of the experiences involved in the conflict. Thus, the psychological meaning of the experiences and the fact of conflict were primary parameters of Freud's earliest theory. Another basic feature of his theory emphasized that symptoms represented compromise solutions of the conflict, solutions which not only preserved both elements of the struggle—the memory of the event and the attempts to obliterate it—but also distorted both.

CHAPTER 5

THE FIRST CONCEPTS AND THE METAPSYCHOLOGICAL VIEWPOINTS DERIVED FROM THEM

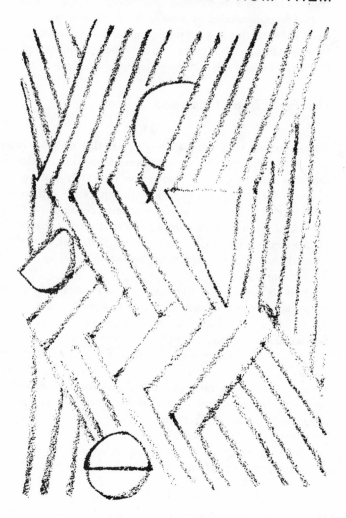

Although Freud's formulations underwent many modifications, the essential orientation that characterizes psychoanalysis and distinguishes it from other psychological approaches to psychopathology and to the study of personality was already established by 1900. That is, prior to the appearance of *The Interpretation of Dreams*, which contains the first major statement of psychoanalytic theory, the unique features of psychoanalysis were already present in some rudimentary form, with one notable exception. There was as yet no theory of motivation by drives, although Freud's mind was indeed prepared to take the conceptual leap demanded by a drive theory once he was coerced by his empirical data. But this interesting turn we will reserve for Chapter 6. Here we pause in our exposition to inspect the basic concepts implied in Freud's first explanations of psychopathological phenomena.

The Early Basic Constructs

There were six basic axiomatic constructs that underlay the explanations Freud offered in his earliest formulations: (1) unconscious mental processes existed; (2) all behavior was ultimately motivated and had meaning; (3) conflict was implicit in all behavior, and there were mental structures such as defenses for mediating conflicts; (4) the past persisted into the present, exerting a steering effect on behavior; (5) quantitative factors underly much of behavior; (6) the behavior of the human organism was not self-determining but was affected by commerce with the real world.

These six factors were all required for an understanding of behavior. None alone proved sufficient. Even today a psychoanalytic explanation must address itself to all six. Although one may not infrequently read psychoanalytic explanations of behavior that regard one or two of these concepts as explanatory—for example, that a symptom can be explained by referring it to a particular conflict or to a particular experience in early life—a comprehensive psychoanalytic point of view sees such attempts at best as incomplete and, probably, as misleading and erroneously simplistic. These six assumptions were later reformulated as six vantage points from which to view behavior, the so-called "metapsychological points of view"—*meta*psychological because no science of behavior had yet embraced all of them simultaneously. Each assumption deserves additional attention. Let us now turn to an examination of each of these concepts.

1. UNCONSCIOUS PSYCHOLOGICAL PROCESSES: THE "TOPOGRAPHIC" POINT OF VIEW OF METAPSYCHOLOGY

The assumption of unconscious psychological processes was not new with Freud. One can trace the idea back at least to Saint Augustine (354–430) who, in his *Confessions* (Augustine, 1955), described how he tried to remember an event from his childhood that eluded his conscious grasp. He knew the memory was still in his mind and yet, simultaneously, outside of it. This is the familiar experience of a temporary forgetting either of significant or inconsequential ideas. Saint Augustine questioned where the ideas were when they were outside of his awareness. Could they be stored somewhere within him, thus existing but not within the grasp of his consciousness?

G. W. Leibniz (1646–1716) introduced another way of regarding nonconscious mental processes. He believed that experience and nature were constructed out of individual elements called *monads*. Monads were indestructible, and although they were individually not perceivable, they combined to form aggregates which were perceivable. Thus a person could not consciously hear a single drop of water in an ocean wave, although the sensation might be unconsciously perceived. The intensity of the registered but not perceived *petites perceptions* was increased by their combining until they could cross a threshold of awareness (Leibniz, 1956).

J. F. Herbart (1776–1841), like Leibniz, concerned himself with a quantitative, or threshold, theory of unconscious processes to solve the problem of what makes an idea conscious at one time and not at another (Herbart, 1891). Leibniz' theory was an arithmetic one; there were experiences of zero intensity, and steady arithmetic additions of *petites perceptions* built up a blend of experiences that attained consciousness. Herbart's theory, on the other hand, emphasized a dynamism among ideas. He assumed that there were conflicts between weak and strong ideas, and weak ideas were *repressed*—kept out of awareness—by strong ones. Unconscious ideas, however, were capable either of combining with or repelling each other, and combinations could attain sufficient strength to challenge the conscious strong ones. Then they could cross the threshold of consciousness. Herbart thus explained the appearance and disappearance of ideas in consciousness by the waxing and waning of the strength of ideas, an oscillation that reflected the combinatory actions of the ideas. In this way, a new experience which was weak, but which was related to a background of previous experience called an *apperceptive mass,* could become conscious. The Herbartian theory regarded the organization of ideas as an active process which can affect conscious experience even while out of consciousness.

G. T. Fechner (1801–1887), whose ideas about the psychology of dreaming were to influence Freud's, formulated a mathematical theory of thresholds buttressed by experimentation on the relationship between increments of stimulus intensity and perceivable sensation. As a threshold conception of awareness, it specifically made room for the existence of unconscious sensations or *negative sensations* (Murphy, 1949).

Hermann von Helmholtz (1821–1894), one of the dominant influences in the physicalist movement, addressed himself to many physiological problems including that of perception. He taught that we perceive objects, not as they impress our sensory organs, but as we infer what they "should be." This "unconscious inference" is based on our past experiences with objects and occurs automatically, without conscious deliberation; therefore, perception is always selective.

Other theories of unconscious processes were not only promulgated at the time Freud was a student but were actually taught to him. Charcot, for example, taught that traumatic paralyses were not the result of brain lesions but of unconscious mental representations. Charcot demonstrated how he could produce these paralyses by hypnosis, although, according to Charcot, hypnosis was a physiological occurrence, an induced disorder of the nervous system.

This brief review should suffice to show that the *concept* of unconscious psychological processes was not new with Freud. The evidence supporting the concept was provided to Freud by two sources: the phenomena of hypnosis and the defective data of consciousness.

As Freud had seen in the demonstrations of posthypnotic phenomena, past experiences could survive in memory and, although unavailable to conscious recall, could continue to exert a steering effect on behavior. Further, in his experience with patients suffering from neurotic symptoms of the defense variety, he was impressed with failures to recall easily many crucial events. But many patients who could not relate what had happened to them could, under hypnosis or firm urging, recall these events. To explain the appearances and disappearances from consciousness of these memories, Freud required a concept of *unconscious psychological processes.*

The methodological problems created by such a concept were not unfamiliar to Freud. He assumed that the problem of inferring unconscious processes was the same as that of inferring conscious processes or of expectancies or sets in animals. He wrote that the world of unconscious psychological processes is "as much unknown to us as the reality of the external world, and it is as incompletely presented by the data of consciousness as is the external world by the communications of our sense organs [1900, p. 613]."

In this manner, he recognized that unconscious psychological processes could only be inferred from conscious thought processes.

> It is true that the physician cannot learn of these unconscious processes until they have produced some effect upon consciousness which can be communicated or observed. But this conscious effect may exhibit a psychological character quite different from that of the unconscious process, so that internal perception cannot possibly regard the one as a substitute for the other. The physician must feel at liberty to proceed by *inference* from the conscious effect to the unconscious psychical process. He thus learns that the conscious effect is only a remote psychical result of the unconscious process, that the latter has not become conscious as such; and moreover that the latter was present and operative even without betraying its existence in any way to consciousness [Freud, 1900, p. 612].

In Freud's view, ideas outside of awareness or without attention paid to them are free to undergo certain transformations, such as linking up with each other in ways that seem illogical and strange or compressing several ideas into one so that there are multiple—even mutually contradictory—connotations of the new entity. Conscious ideas, moreover, tend to maintain their logical relationship with other conscious ideas. Ideas which remain outside of consciousness are by that fact disposed to a fate different from that of those in awareness. Another distinction to be kept in mind is that Freud, in contrast to Herbart, regarded the unconscious ideas as powerful and dominant.

2: BEHAVIOR IS MOTIVATED: THE "DYNAMIC" POINT OF VIEW OF METAPSYCHOLOGY

As early as 1893, when what was to become the introduction to the "Studies on Hysteria" was published as a separate paper, Freud stated this basic axiom of the psychoanalytic approach: Behavior is lawful, it is caused, and it serves purposes.

> A chance observation has led us, over a number of years, to investigate a great variety of different forms and symptoms of hysteria, with a view to discovering their precipitating causes—the event which provoked the first occurrence, often many years earlier, of the phenomenon in question. In the great majority of cases it is not possible to establish the point of origin by a simple interrogation of the patient, however thoroughly it may be carried out. This is in part because what is in question is often some experience which the patient dislikes discussing; but principally because he is genuinely unable to recollect it and often has no suspicion of the cause or connection between the precipitating event and the pathological phenomenon. . . . *Our experiences have shown us, however, that the most various symptoms which are ostensibly spontaneous and, as one might say, idiopathic products of hysteria, are just as strictly related to the precipitating trauma as the phenomena to which we have just alluded and which exhibit the connection quite clearly* [Breuer & Freud, 1893, pp. 3–4].

The examples of cause and effect Freud and Breuer offered were clear enough. For example:

> A highly intelligent man was present while his brother had an ankylosed hip joint extended under an anesthetic. The instant at which the joint gave way with a crack, he felt a violent pain in his own hip joint which persisted for nearly a year [1893, p. 5].

In other cases the connection was less clear and seemed more of an attribution. "For instance a neuralgia may follow upon mental pain [1893, p. 5]," an insistent feeling of moral revulsion was suppressed but was followed by nausea and vomiting.

But in the long run, as Hume argued (1901), cause and effect relationships are established in the eyes of the observer. They represent his belief, his attribution of cause to a sequence of events. Freud's causal statements described both the patient's present purposes achieved by his behavior as well as earlier causes of that behavior. Statements about motives and purposes, therefore, are typical of the psychoanalytic approach. Freud attributed neurotic meaning not only to neurotic symptoms but to apparently inconsequential behaviors of everyday life (called *parapraxes*)—slips of the tongue, momentary forgetting, errors in actions, mislaying of objects and, above all, dreams.

The forgetting of intentions can in general be traced to an opposing current of thought, which is unwilling to carry out the intention. But this view is not only held by us psychoanalysts; it is the general opinion, accepted by everyone in their daily lives and only denied when it comes to theory. A patron who gives his *protégé* the excuse of having forgotten his request fails to justify himself. The *protégé* immediately thinks: "It means nothing to him; it's true he promised, but he doesn't really want to do it."

You will no doubt find it incredible that we ourselves can play an intentional part in what is so often the painful accident of losing something. . . . We lose an object if we have quarreled with the person who gave it to us and do not want to be reminded of him; or if we no longer like the object itself and want to have an excuse for getting another and better one instead. The same intention directed against an object can also play a part, of course, in cases of dropping, breaking or destroying things. . . . A youngish man told me the following story: "Some years ago there were misunderstandings between me and my wife. I found her too cold, and although I willingly recognized her excellent qualities we lived together without any tender feelings. One day, returning from a walk, she gave me a book which she had bought because she thought it would interest me. I thanked her for this mark of attention, promised to read the book and put it on one side. After that I could never find it again. Months passed by, in which I occasionally remembered the lost book and made vain attempts to find it. About six months later my dear mother, who was not living with us, fell ill. My wife left home to nurse her mother-in-law. The patient's condition became serious and gave my wife an opportunity of showing the best side of herself. One evening I returned home full of enthusiasm and gratitude for what my wife had accomplished. I walked up to my desk, and without any definite intention but with a kind of somnambulistic certainty opened one of the drawers. On the very top I found the long-lost book I had mislaid." With the extinction of the motive the mislaying of the object ceased as well [1901; 1916–1917, pp. 53, 55].

Thus motives are active not only in the formation of new symptoms but in much of our everyday behavior. The causal laws of symptom formation are not qualitatively different from the causal laws of non-neurotic behavior.

This view of behavior has often been misunderstood. Some have ascribed to psychoanalysis the search for a single motive or intention in behavior. The psychoanalytic approach, however, emphasizes not only the plurality of motives in a sample of behavior but the involvement of the other five metapsychological points of view presented in this chapter. Although it is rarely possible to discover and isolate all of them, a hierarchy of motives is always involved.

Psychoanalysis does not, however, insist on which motives are primary in any behavior, for that is an empirical question and one which in the history of psychoanalysis has had different answers. In the early years of psychoanalytic investigations, as we have seen, the principal motives for hysteria and obsessional symptoms appeared to be the memory of an unbearably painful experience involving sexual seduction, generally by a parent. As we shall see in Chapter 6, Freud learned that his patients' reports of incestuous relations were not in accord with the real facts. Yet patients continued to tell him tales of sexual seductions, forcing Freud to conclude that these stories were fantasies that reflected the existence of sexual motives in the patients. Further, the analysis of dreams led him to respect the power of wishes, particularly sexual ones, deriving from the early years of life. These encounters with patients' fantasies drew his attention to the sexual drive in man. The motivational role of the sexual drive in its protean forms was given careful study, but it was not considered the exclusive motivator of behavior. Later, self-preservative motives, motives of mastery, self-regard, and aggression were also scrutinized and given a place in the psychoanalytic theory of motivation.

Thus, the point of view that behavior was motivated had both conceptual and empirical roots. The conceptual root stemmed from the physicalist tradition, which forced him to look for antecedent causes and lawful relationships. But for Freud, the causes were not solely mechanistic; they could also be purposive. The empirical roots of this point of view were in the observations of his patients and their verbal reports of early experiences. These were later to be supplemented, complemented, and revised by direct observations and psychoanalyses of children.

3. CONFLICT IS IMPLICIT IN ALL BEHAVIOR, AND THERE ARE MENTAL STRUCTURES FOR MEDIATING CONFLICTS: THE "STRUCTURAL" POINT OF VIEW OF METAPSYCHOLOGY

Freud's observations were made on patients suffering from neurotic complaints, and in this admittedly biased sample of human behavior, he observed the ubiquitous presence of conflicts. He was impressed with his patients' struggles to obliterate painful recollections and, during the treatment itself, with their strenuous efforts not to remember. The psychology of conflict thus became a key issue in psychoanalysis. One may well agree with Waelder (1937; 1960, p. 9), who regarded the uniqueness of psychoanalysis as viewing human behavior from the perspective of conflict. The theoretical nature of the forms of conflict, however, underwent many changes. As we have seen, at first Freud defined the basic neurotic conflict as one between the memory of a real event and the patient's moral requirements of himself. Later the conflict was conceptualized as one between manifestations of drives—for example, of a sexual drive—and controlling structures, like defenses. Still other conflicts were studied, such as those between (a) reality constraints and drives (as in the development of self-control), (b) reality and self-regard (as in feelings of shame), and (c) manifestations of conscience and one's overt behavior (as in feelings of guilt).

The status of conflict in all behavior is illustrated in the explanation of slips of the tongue and in dreams. In slips, for example, Freud assumed that the conflict occurs between two antithetical intentions, one of which is unconscious. The compromise between them results in the parapraxis.

> We are told that a lady who was well known for her energy remarked on one occasion: "My husband asked his doctor what diet he ought to follow; but the doctor told him he had no need to diet: he could eat and drink what I want [Freud, 1916–1917, p. 35]."

Freud added:

> What we have before us are corrections, additions or continuations, by means of which a second purpose makes itself felt alongside of the first. . . . "My husband can eat and drink what he wants. But, as you know, *I*

don't put up with wanting anything at all, so he can eat and drink what *I* want [1916–1917, pp. 62–63]."

In this example we can see illustrated some of the essential variables in the Freudian theory of conflict. In addition to the two intentions, there is the further assumption that one of these intentions has met with a resistance to its expression. The resisted intention, however, continues to exert a force towards expression, even though it is held in abeyance and out of awareness. There are also certain assumed conditions for the rejection of this otherwise gratifying intention, such as fear of punishment, social disapproval, or the power of the intention itself lest it get out of hand. These countermotives represent a pleasure-pain spectrum and, as such, the conflict within the person. That is, *both* elements of the conflict are gratifying and pain-producing—in different ways—to the person. Neither element represents only gratification or denial of gratification. Neither element of the conflict alone sufficiently explains the behavior, and with merely one element present, there is no conflict.

A psychology that focuses on conflict as a central human experience requires a theory of the structure of the conflicting elements. In psychoanalysis these elements were conceptualized—before 1900—as traumatic experiences versus an idealized self-concept. *After 1900 the hypothetical elements of conflict became wishes or drives versus psychological defensive structures of thought.* From its earliest beginnings, then, the psychoanalytic view encompassed not only urges or drives, but controlling and modulating structures. These thought structures permitted the substitution of a kind of experimental thought-action for motor action which was urged by drive forces. These structures were presumed to have a developmental dimension, for in the course of maturation, the child learns to tame and direct the urging from his drives by using such functions as memory, concentration, and attention. In postulating these control structures, then, psychoanalysis has had to concern itself with the psychology of defense, of thought processes such as memory, attention, and perception, as well as with drive manifestations such as fantasy and affect.

In the psychoanalytic view, the changing form of conflicts, too, has a developmental dimension. What in early childhood may have been a conflict between an internal impulse and an external parental prohibition may later become automatically reenacted without the presence of the external provocation. Such internalized conflicts are presumed to have the status of a totally *intra*psychic conflict. Thus the conflict point of view required the assumption that social constraints become internalized. *How* they become internalized was not to be a concern of psychoanalytic theory until the 1920s (see Chapter 9).

Another aspect of the conflict point of view bears on the clinical theory. In his search for psychological explanations of neurotic behavior, Freud attempted to isolate specific impulse-defense patterns for each neurosis, particularly for those he called the defense neuropsychoses (1894, 1896). These formulations underwent many changes. Attempts to describe specific conflicts as the sole etiological factors in specific psychopathological conditions can never be wholly successful, for they can account for only one aspect of the psychopathology. In one of Freud's papers, for example, he discussed the etiology of a paranoid psychosis (1911) and came to the conclusion that latent homosexual conflicts played a leading part in the development of the psychosis. But whether latent homosexual conflicts underlie all paranoid conditions is an empirical question. Contrary evidence about the etiological role of specific conflicts in specific psychopathological disorders will not weaken the *general* theory. For the general theory calls merely for granting conflict a crucial role in behavior and psychopathology.

4. THE PAST PERSISTS INTO THE PRESENT: THE "GENETIC" POINT OF VIEW OF METAPSYCHOLOGY

The pre-1900 explanation of hysterical symptoms focused on the patient's experiences prior to the outbreak of the neurosis. Freud, the reader will recall, was able to trace the historical circumstances of the patient's neurotic pattern back to childhood. Thus, a reported seduction that happened at the age of seventeen, which was followed by attacks of hysterical symptoms, derived exaggerated significance for the patient because it appeared to repeat a similar event that had occurred earlier in the life of the patient.

Although this "seduction" theory of etiology was soon abandoned, the formal nature of that theory continues as one of the hallmarks of a psychoanalytic explanation. The psychoanalysis of an event or a symptom consists partly in tracing back one aspect of behavior—whether thought, action, or affect—to another which preceded it and out of which it appears to have developed. But past experiences could rarely be the sole necessary conditions for the development of psychopathology. It is not simply the past legacy of experience that gives significance to the present but, in Freud's view, a mutual interaction between and integration of constitutional factors and environmental events. The former consists of the disposition and strength of drives, constitutional endowments and capacities; the latter consists of experiences that impinge on the person from the social-physical-environmental field. Neither factor predominates. The amalgam, however, determines the nature of subsequent experience. To that extent, we may say that the past continues into the present and exerts determining effects on behavior. The genetic point of view thus gives a historical context to contemporary existence and, in this way, gives meaning, significance, and uniqueness to the understanding of a life.

The alloying of constitutional and environmental factors may be regarded as a way in which integrative solutions have been arrived at. Consider a vigorously intrusive and curious child whose explorations and intrusiveness reflect a particularly strong drive. Suppose he is compelled to abort his curiosity under threat of loss of his parents' love. The history of how that child will modulate and express his intrusiveness and curiosity will be different from that of a sibling with a less vigorous urge. Indeed it will be different from that of a friend whose drive strength may be similar but whose parents are more permissive, encouraging, or perhaps disinterested.

The solution to the drive-control conflict arrived at during childhood will persist. If that solution should implicate a control that inhibits the child's curiosity, then inhibition of curiosity may be typical for this child on through adolescence and into his adulthood. And, to continue the hypothetical example, should he develop a learning difficulty, the psychoanalytic explanation of that symptom will take account of the historical context of such inhibitions of intrusiveness and curiosity.

This view that previously arrived-at solutions continue into the present also underlies the explanation of what has been called regressive behavior—the emergence, under some conditions, of previously superseded but still latent and potential behavior, such as temper tantrums, infantile dependence, or enuresis.

5. QUANTITATIVE FACTORS UNDERLIE MUCH OF BEHAVIOR: THE "ECONOMIC" POINT OF VIEW OF METAPSYCHOLOGY

The earliest observations of psychoanalysis centered on the neuroses; there one becomes struck by the power of intrusive ideas and of compulsive acts in obsessional and compulsive conditions, of the strength of delusional ideas in paranoid states, and of the intractability to medical intervention of conversion phenomena in hysterical states. The first psychoanalytic explanations posited that affects were "displaced" from the memory of an unbearable experience on to other, previously neutral ideas, thus weakening that formerly painful memory but perhaps strengthening the other less painful ideas beyond rational expectations. Likewise in the psychotherapy of these conditions, Freud reported the quantity of *resistance* that patients manifested against free recall of experiences, in spite of their firm resolution to cooperate. These observations, which imply quantities—for example, of affect and of resistance —forced Freud to postulate a hypothetical quantity in behavior. Although in 1894 he had not identified the quantity, it later evolved into quantities of drive and degrees of control over drive. Drives can vary in strength and so can the modulating and controlling structures.

This quantitative point of view is perhaps one of the more controversial within psychoanalysis. Freud was never totally satisfied with his quantitative formulations, and neither are most analysts. But the assumption of quantitative factors underlying the strength of drives, affects, structural controls, and such phenomena as displacement and condensation (see Chapter 7) seems to be necessary whether or not one can identify the quantities as psychological energies. Consider one of the many observations on which Freud based his theory of self-regard or of narcissism. A person falls ill and suffers intense organic pain. His interest diminishes in both his surrounding world of objects and in his important loved ones. "So long as he suffers he ceases to love [Freud, 1914b]." The familiar self-centeredness of the sick person is described here in quantitative terms as the ebb and flow of interest in the painful part of his body and in his personal, ambient world of things and people.

6. COMMERCE WITH THE REAL WORLD IS A DETERMINING FACTOR OF BEHAVIOR: THE "ADAPTIVE" POINT OF VIEW OF METAPSYCHOLOGY

This principle has been conceptualized by Rapaport and Gill (1967) as the *adaptive point of view*. The early theory considered the nature of reality only to the extent that it represented factors that impinged upon the organism; reality conveyed trauma, frustrations, and interferences with growth. The theory did not then concern itself with the opportunities for growth and the positive shaping of behavior offered by the social milieu. When, however, the psychoanalytic drive theory was formulated after 1900, reality was considered in the theory insofar as it offered need-satisfying objects for drives. Thus, a postulated hunger drive in a very young infant whose site of action is the mouth and alimentary canal and which involves mouthing actions requires for its satisfaction the real presence of a need-satisfying object: appropriate food and appropriate handling. The maturing drives require a changing series of objects. In later editions of the theory, the nature of the objects and the way they do or do not meet and satisfy the drives have a shaping effect on the development of behavior, character, and psychopathology.

In later psychoanalytic considerations, the contribution of reality to development was conceptualized not merely as providing a need-satisfying object but as a series of "average expectable environments" (Erikson, 1963; Hartmann, 1939) to which adaptation is required. That is, the biological equipment of the organism at one age requires for survival a range of possibilities for nurturing the growth of the organism. As the organism matures, different environments are required. The biological equipment of the organism "fits in" with a range of "expectable" environments which include physical and social features. In the psychoanalytic view, therefore, an understanding of behavior demands an understanding of both the physical and the social reality which form part of the life experiences of a particular person. This point of view of reality may be regarded as an ultimately biological one rather than a basically sociological one, for it emphasizes a Darwinian adaptational point of view. In this view behavior is to be understood neither as a passive response to environmental press nor as impelled by autonomous drive forces. The psychosocial factors claim equal recognition with drives.

These six characteristics of the psychoanalytic viewpoint, then, comprise the special outlook of psychoanalysis on behavior. In the following chapters we will trace their development and try to show their importance for an understanding of psychopathology in particular and of some more general aspects of behavior not considered psychopathological.

Summary

Freud's earliest formulations were based on six assumptions which still remain distinguishing features of the psychoanalytic edifice and which comprise its *metapsychology:* (1) unconscious mental processes exist (the topographic point of view); (2) behavior is motivated (the dynamic point of view); (3) conflict is implicit in all behavior, and there are mental structures for mediating conflicts (the structural point of view); (4) the past persists into the present (the genetic point of view); (5) quantitative factors underlie much of behavior (the economic point of view); and (6) interaction with the real world affects behavior (the adaptive point of view). All six points of view would be required for a complete psychoanalytic understanding of behavior.

CHAPTER 6

THE FIRST REVISIONS

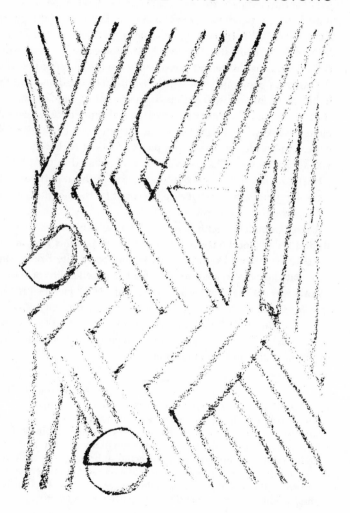

Discarding the "Seduction" Theory

With continuing clinical practice, Freud became wary of the literal truth of his female patients' reports of actual seductions by their fathers or uncles. Yet the persistence of these reports in the life histories of his patients puzzled him. He was also bewildered when he considered that if incestuous experiences were so common, illnesses resulting from them were so rare. What were the conditions that contributed to the establishment of a neurosis? The theory of etiology he had arrived at with Breuer held that hysterical symptoms were the result of sexual trauma, the affective components of which had been blocked and had therefore to be forced into unusual outlets, such as bodily complaints and conversion symptoms. The theory regarded actual experiences as causal. In his clinical work, when Freud traced the memory of the trauma back to the patient's past life, he uncovered recollections of earlier and still earlier sexual experiences. That sexuality was implicated in the illness of hysterical patients seemed incontestable. But if the reports of seductions were not literally true, what could account for the fact that patients kept talking as if they were true?

Biased sampling techniques were first considered. In Freud's case studies a disproportionately large number of patients may indeed have actually experienced seductions. A second possibility Freud considered was that the reports were untrue, for the unreliability of retrospective reports was appreciated then as now. Still a third factor—his own introspections—led Freud to begin to doubt the authenticity of the reports. He had begun to analyze himself and was astonished to find in himself similar ideas. In August, 1897 he wrote an account of his reasoning to his friend Wilhelm Fliess in Berlin:

I will confide in you at once the great secret that has been slowly dawning on me in the last few months. I no longer believe in my *neurotica* (theory of the neuroses). This is probably not intelligible without an explanation; after all, you yourself found what I could tell you credible. So I will begin historically from the question of the origin of my reasons for disbelief. The continual disappointments in my attempts at bringing my analysis to a real conclusion, the running-away of people who had for a time seemed most in my grasp, the absence of the complete successes on which I had reckoned, the possibility of explaining the partial successes in other ways, on ordinary lines,—this was the first group. Then came surprise at the fact that in every case the father, not excluding my own, had to be blamed as a pervert—the realization of the unexpected frequency of hysteria, in which the same determinant is invariably established, though such a widespread extent of perversity towards children is, after all, not very probable. (The perversity would have to be immeasurably more frequent than the hysteria, since the illness only arises where there has been an accumulation of events and where a factor that weakens defence has supervened.) . . . I have no idea now where I have got to, since I have not achieved a theoretical understanding of repression and its interplay of forces. It seems to have become once again arguable that it is only later experiences that give impetus to phantasies, which then hark back to childhood; and with this the factor of a hereditary disposition regains a sphere of influence from which I had made it my task to expel it—in the interest of throwing a flood of light on neurosis [1892–1899, pp. 259–260].

That Freud did not despair in spite of the fact that his theory proved wrong is a measure of his remarkable scientific integrity. The theory was expendable, but the data were not. His patients had indeed told him about seduction experiences, and Freud himself had had such recollections. The data to be explained, then, must be the tales of seductions rather than the seductions themselves, which Freud could no longer accept as actually having occurred. He reasoned that the seductions so strongly presented in the course of treatment must be fantasied reconstructions rather than descriptions of actual events. If these experiences had not actually occurred, one was forced to explain the striking frequency of the fantasies. The explanation was sought from a study of the psychological experiences of the sexual development of children, a development in which constitutional-biological, as well as psychological and social, factors were present. Many years later, in reviewing the changes in his ideas, Freud described his dawning awareness of the role of these fantasies in his patients' lives:

When this etiology [the seduction hypothesis] broke down under its own improbability and under contradiction in definitely ascertainable circumstances, the result at first was helpless bewilderment. Analysis had led by the right paths back to these sexual dramas, and yet they were not true. Reality was lost from under one's feet. At that time I would gladly have given up the whole thing just as my esteemed predecessor, Breuer, had done when he made his unwelcome discovery. Perhaps I persevered only because I had no choice and could not then begin at anything else. At last came the reflection that, after all, one has no right to despair because one has been deceived in one's expectations; one must revise them. If hysterics trace back their symptoms to fictitious traumas, this new fact signifies that they create such scenes in fantasy, and psychical reality requires to be taken into account alongside actual reality. This was soon followed by the recognition that these fantasies were intended to cover up the autoerotic activity of early childhood, to gloss it over and raise it to a higher level; and then behind the fantasies, the whole range of the child's sexual life came to light [1914c, p. 17].

The Role of Fantasies

Freud now introduced three important modifications into the theory: (1) Reports of the infantile sexual traumas were considered to be fantasies; (2) the fantasies were considered to be effects of a sexual drive; and (3) the search for an actual exciting cause was abandoned in favor of explaining the ways in which the patient's sexual disposition, already present in childhood, expressed itself in behavior and in his consequent reactions to his infantile sexual experiences. This third modification had a critical effect on the technique of psychoanalytic therapy, for the sexual motivations and the modulation of and defense against their expression became the focus of therapeutic scrutiny. With no postulation of actual traumatic experiences in the patients' lives, constitutional, biological factors acquired a firmer position in the explanation of neurosis. These constitutional factors, however, were not of the same sort as Charcot's "degenerative predisposition" to neurosis. As Freud put it, "Thus it was no longer a question of what sexual experiences a particular individual had in his childhood, but rather of his reaction to those experiences [1906, pp. 276–277]." The illness was to be viewed as an outcome of a conflict between sexual motivations and defenses against them, a conflict with roots that reached back into the child's early development and which left traces in the form of fantasies.

The major theoretical papers in which the new theory was blocked out were not, strictly speaking, those concerned with psychopathology. Freud directed his attention for many months to the phenomena of dreams and of everyday errors, such as forgetting, slips of the tongue, and erroneous acts—phenomena that occur daily to all people, whether or not they are patients. The ingenious analyses of these behaviors permitted Freud to construct a theory of the psychic apparatus and a model of the mind which, although subsequently modified in many respects, remains as a rich source of hypotheses about behavior. Clinical pathological case studies were also used by Freud as basic data for theory construction, but normal behavior—dreams and errors—was also a principal base of observations, providing much of the raw data for his theory-building. Theoretical papers about psychopathology were firmly based upon his ideas about normal behavior, that is, upon the principles of mental functioning he had postulated from his observations of dreams and errors, and vice versa.

For example, in his first published case history following the appearance of "Studies on Hysteria" (Breuer & Freud, 1893–1895), Freud carefully, and with great subtlety, analyzed a case of hysteria (Freud, 1905a). He called the patient "Dora." The case study revolves about the analysis of two of Dora's dreams; from them Freud was able to extract many essential elements that contributed to her neurosis. Dora was a rather sullen and angry eighteen-year-old girl who developed a nervous cough and a hysterical *aphonia*. Her parents were unhappily married, and her father began an affair with the wife of his friend, Herr K. For her part, Frau K. took a warm interest in Dora. Dora's mother turned all of her attention to housecleaning with such intensity that no one could enjoy the fruits of her efforts. Herr K., however, became sexually attracted to Dora and began to propose marriage to her; she slapped his face and demanded that her parents break off their friendship with the K. family. The two dreams of Dora that are the focus of this case study depict her sexual feelings for her father, for Herr K., and also for Frau K., although she was unaware of those feelings. The essence of this case study is an exploration of the similarities between the formation of dreams and of neuroses.

A major methodological position thus emerges: *neurotic, psychotic, and normal behavior are not discontinuous;* rather, the structure of the mental apparatus and the nature of the motivations are similar, regardless of the presence of psychopathology. He wrote that neurotic mechanisms are not created by the impact of pathological disturbances upon the mind; they are already present in the normal structure of the mind.

Slips and Errors

Freud's interest in dreams as a psychological phenomenon extended back many years prior to the publication of *The Interpretation of Dreams* in 1900. His interest was both in the *meaning* of dreams and in a theory to explain how they originate. Likewise, slips and errors presented themselves to him as meaningful behavior through which a person expressed his conflicting intentions. Freud's method for discovering such intentions was simply to ask the person to suspend judgment on his thoughts and to let associations to the act freely enter his mind. His book *The Psychopathology of Everyday Life* (1901) is filled with interesting illustrations and demonstrations of the intentional nature of the human errors to be found in ordinary day-to-day living.

Here is an example of such a slip of the tongue drawn from actual contemporary clinical practice. A patient discovered in the course of his social contacts that his analyst had been divorced for several years. During an analytic session he mentioned this and rebuked his analyst for not being able to keep his own life in order, the proof of which, the patient said, was that the analyst was "devoiced." Associations to this slip of the tongue revealed that it was a condensation of divorce and voice and that it expressed (1) the patient's irritation with the analyst for not being the perfect parent and for being like his own father who could not get along with his mother; (2) the patient's reproach to the analyst for not confiding in the patient and for forcing the patient to learn about the analyst through the medium of a third party; (3) the patient's belief that the analyst had no interest in sharing things with the patient but instead kept silent (i.e., without voice), although the patient realized that the analyst was not there to share his problems with the patient; and (4) the gratification the patient derived from the analyst's voice which, like his mother's, soothed him in times of stress.

Freud's explanation for such acts began with the assumption that they were purposeful. If one accepts the assumption that these are meaningful acts, one can discern in them at least two intentions, one of which is outside of the awareness of the person. The intentions have a force and a direction, but one of them has been rejected from consciousness and direct expression because if it were expressed, the person (1) would risk social disapproval, (2) would risk self-castigation, and (3) would fear the power of the intention itself. These motives for suppression explicitly state that the conflict is an internal one and that the act has meaning within the historical context of the person (for, after all, what is embarrassing to him may not be to his friend). It also presumes that people censor their thoughts and activities and that such censoring may go on outside of awareness.

Such acts require a conceptualization of the mind that explains the "how" of such internal conflicts and their resolution. This model was worked out in great detail in Freud's masterpiece *The Interpretation of Dreams* (1900, ch. VII). In that volume, Freud refers to matters which are outside of awareness as being "unconscious." As a translation of the German *unbewusst*, the term unconscious has a double meaning: first, the idea is unconscious in the sense that it is out of awareness; second, the person who has the idea is unconscious—unaware—of it.

The term in psychoanalysis also has a double meaning: a descriptive as well as a dynamic meaning. Descriptively, it refers to any idea outside of awareness, including ideas which at the moment are not conscious but can become conscious with only slight effort, like one's phone number. Dynamically, however, it refers to those ideas which are blocked from easy access to awareness, like the unconscious intention in the slip of the tongue.

Since patients often spoke of their dreams during the course of their psychotherapeutic interviews, Freud assumed that, like all other productions, these dreams had meaning and significance. Such an assumption differed from most explanations of dreaming current in the 1890s, for dreams were generally regarded either as meaningless or as solely somatic phenomena. By contrast, Freud regarded dreams as the activity of the mind while the person was asleep. That the mind continues such activity during sleep indicates that some stimulus is continuing to act upon it and, thus, to disturb it. Dreams, therefore, Freud assumed, were to be viewed as the reaction of the mind to stimuli active during sleep, and the strange character of dreams was to be attributed to the fact that the person is in a state of sleep rather than one of alert wakefulness. He wrote that dreams reflect the reaction of the mind to stimuli during sleep.

Dreams

Because Freud regarded dreams as thought products that occur during an altered state of consciousness, he was obliged to study the properties of dreams. He believed that the nature of mental functioning in general can be learned best from a study of extreme phenomena such as dreams or symptoms. Freud's first approach was a thorough description of the dream as a phenomenon; then each of the characteristics of dream thinking would have to be explained within a theory of mind. The mind's mode of reaction is indeed peculiarly different during sleep.

1. Although some—and perhaps much—of the dream experience may be coherent and comprehensible, much of it is incoherent and strange. A dream figure, for example, may appear as a familiar person, yet simultaneously have the qualities of two other people. Scenes may shift without logical reason: a person long dead may appear, thus violating the strictures of time.

2. The dream is a highly sensory experience with emphasis on visual qualities, although other sense modalities, particularly audition, may be involved. This sensory, hallucinatory quality imparts contemporaneity to the dream thoughts: whatever in reality took place in the past seems in the dream to be taking place now.

3. Should there be an external stimulus actually impinging on the sleeper, that stimulus is transformed in the dream into something only remotely related to it.[1]

4. Contemporary events can be discerned in dreams. This is particularly so for events that the dreamer experienced earlier that day or the previous day.

These four characteristics of dreams—(1) their incoherence or illogicality, (2) their hallucinatory vividness and timelessness, (3) the transformations of stimuli, and (4) the representation of some elements of the previous day—testify to the different nature of the thought process during dreaming. An explanation of dreams must take into account these four factors.

THE MEANING OF DREAMS

But what might be the meaning of dreams? More specifically, what might be the nature of the disturbing stimuli? Freud's search for an answer to these questions, as to all other mental phenomena, followed this

---

[1] For example, one of the earliest dream experimenters, Maury (1857), arranged to have his nose and lips tickled with a feather while he slept. He dreamed that a mask was pasted on his face and was then peeled off, ripping his skin with it. In another experiment, a pair of scissors was rubbed against a pair of pliers. He dreamed of pealing bells.

approach: if someone tells you something and you fail to understand it, ask him to explain it. When his patients told him of their dreams, Freud asked them to tell him the meaning of the dreams. He also analyzed his own dreams by this same technique. Though his patients did not consciously know the meaning of their dreams, Freud thought that such meaning could be found. The technique of free association became the technique for studying the meaning of the dream, although by no means was the meaning inevitably discovered. In this approach, then, dreams are considered to be representations of thoughts of which the dreamer is (momentarily) unaware. Freud referred to the actual dreams as the *manifest dream;* the thoughts for which the dream served as a substitute he termed the *latent dream thoughts.* The manifest dream is a pictorial representation of the latent dream thoughts. These latent dream thoughts are arrived at through the technique of free association. Attempts to track them down through this technique, however, inevitably meet various forms of resistance such as skepticism, minimizing of the significance of thoughts, or blocking. Since in dreams an intention (the latent thought) comes into conflict with opposing forces (the resistances), Freud could classify dreams with other psychic phenomena, such as errors, as compromises intended to resolve psychic conflict.

CHILDREN'S DREAMS

Freud noted that young children's dreams were less distorted and subjected to fewer transformations than were those of adults. Through such dreams Freud was able to extract their significance and then to extrapolate his conclusions to the dreams of adults. He discerned six characteristics of children's dreams:

1. There is always in the dream some event drawn from the previous day, an event which appears to explain the dream. Among the many examples he gives is the following:

A girl of three and a quarter years was taken across the lake for the first time. At the landing stage she did not want to leave the boat and wept bitterly. The crossing had been too short for her. The next morning she announced, "Last night I went on the lake." We may safely add that this crossing lasted longer [1916–1917, p. 127].

2. The latent dream thought seems quite congruent with the manifest dream with only minimal disguising of the latent dream thought.

3. The stimulus for the dream is assumed to be a disturbing wish, a wish that remained unsatisfied in waking life but which was directly gratified in the dream—for example, in the previous illustration, to continue the boat trip. Freud, therefore, considered the dream to be a response to the stimulus of the unsatisfied wish.

4. Since dreams are a reaction to a mental stimulus, their purpose is to remove that excitation so that sleep can continue. Dreams, then, are to be regarded as preservers rather than disturbers of sleep. The unfulfilled wish is the ultimate disturber of sleep.

5. The dream represents the wish as fulfilled. The little girl is actually sailing in her dream. The hallucination, by its concrete sensory imagery, represents the thought in the present tense. In thus transforming the thought into a current percept, the dream allows the thoughts to be worked over, reexperienced, and subsequently discarded.

6. Just as the analysis of errors showed a conflict between two tendencies, so Freud's scrutiny of dreams revealed a conflict between a disturbing and a disturbed tendency. The former appears as the latent dream thought and the latter as the desire to remain undisturbed by it and, thereby, to sleep. A compromise between these two tendencies results in the dream. The disturbing stimulus will of course vary with the preoccupations of the sleeper, but the desire to sleep is omnipresent.

Thus, from an examination of children's dreams which are without much distortion, Freud concluded that dreams are to be regarded as mental rather than physical phenomena, that they have meaning, that they represent a conflict between a disturbing thought or wish and the desire to sleep, that they represent the wish as fulfilled through the agency of a hallucinatory experience.[2]

Although distortion is not an inevitable characteristic of dreams—for many children's dreams are undisguised—it is typical of dreams from later childhood on. Unusual representations and images occur in the dreams of adults. The typical distortions of adults' dreams, however, do not prevent those dreams from being understood. They simply make the task of understanding the dreams more complex. To explain the distortions in dreams, Freud assumed the operation of a distorting mechanism

[2] Later, in a revision of the theory of dreams, Freud regarded dreams as *attempts* at wish fulfillment.

which he called the *dream work* which transformed the latent dream thoughts in certain ways. These included omissions, displacements of accent, and general modifications of the order of the material. Freud considered that the dream work was motivated by a need to censor unwelcome thoughts and desires. He described the censorship anthropomorphically as an agent—indeed as a homunculus—and intended this description as a metaphor to clarify the concept of a relationship between hypothetical, but conflicting, mental forces: forbidden wishes (the unmodified dream thoughts) that conflicted with the person's ideals, for the sake of which he must renounce those urges. Thus, a monitoring function provides a watchfulness over those wishes. The functions of this watchfulness and censorship are usually consistent with the conscious judgment of the dreamer about himself, although at times ideals of which he is unaware may also prod the censorship. Whether or not the ideals are conscious, there is an assumed critical standard against which the person judges himself and for the sake of which moral discrepancies are resolved by the censorship function.

DREAM WISHES

The model of the psychic apparatus developed from a study of dreams is in most respects the same as that developed in Chapter 4. The conflicting agencies, however, are changed. Rather than censorship being rallied by the person's ethical standards against memories of repugnant events, it was now aimed at the person's own wishes which are found to be objectionable. What are these forbidden wishes? The identification of these desires is an empirical matter, and Freud's clinical experience and his analysis of his own dreams forced upon him the recognition of some of them. Their hierarchical importance shifted with his clinical experiences, as we will see in Chapter 8, but their essence remained essentially unmodified. They represent wishes to gratify one's sexual impulses on objects generally forbidden by society—particularly incestuous choices. The mode by which sexual gratification would be sought in one's wishes may be contrary to that permitted by one's self or by society. But not only sexual urges, with their search for affectionate bonds, are represented in these forbidden wishes; hate, destruction, and vengeance against those loved most may also appear. These wishes, the psychological representation of biological urges, can become active and because of their abhorrent qualities have to be censored. Dreams, then, represent the transformation of these wishes by the dream work at the behest of the censorship function.

Dream distortion is thus to be explained as the outcome of a censorship of desires that are offensive to a person's ideals and self-representations. These offensive desires are kept out of awareness by censorship during the day; the special circumstances that permit their entrance into consciousness at night, even disguised as a dream, are the focus of a theoretical argument by Freud which we will discuss in Chapter 7.

A study of the ways in which the latent dream thoughts are transformed into the dream led to a mapping of thought modes that seemed strange to those who assumed that logical thought patterns were the only kind of thinking characteristic of man. The dream work which transforms the latent content into the manifest dream was seen by Freud to be the reverse work of dream interpretation. To unravel the hieroglyphics of the dream in interpretation is to undo the dream work, retranslating the text into the original language of the latent dream thoughts.

THE DREAM WORK

Four processes of the dream work may be distinguished: *condensation, displacement, visual imagery,* and *secondary revision.*

1. *Condensation.* This refers to the finding that the dream is always more laconic and terse than the meaning it contains. Interpretative work always unravels multiple strands. In particular, single images in a dream can represent several latent elements. Thus a figure may look like one's father, yet act like one's teacher, and still the dreamer is convinced that it is the brother of his good friend. The latent meaning of this condensation can be discerned in the common characteristics of the three people. Such condensations occur with objects and places as well as with people. Since multiple meanings of a dream image often elude the dreamer, the censorship function often makes use of condensation for purposes of disguise. If this sounds too anthropomorphic, it can be restated: the purposes of censorship can be served by condensation, although the condensation is not to be construed as a mechanism of the censorship. Many times the elements that combine are strange to each other, and the composite appears bizarre.

2. *Displacement.* This refers to the shift of accent in a dream from something important to something unimportant or remote or from an objectionable to an unobjectionable thought. This shift of accent was regarded by Freud as having a defensive or censoring function. Here is an example of displacement in a patient's dream. This patient was experiencing great difficulty in acknowledging to himself that the interviews with his analyst were important to him. He had always found it impossible to let himself feel that anyone could be important to him. He dreamed that something had gotten under his skin. "A friend who examined me mentioned several kinds of skin diseases as diagnoses. He also mentioned something about a cardiac condition." The "heart condition" received only casual mention in the patient's account of the dream, but the work of interpretation showed it to be central in the patient's concerns. The analyst had indeed gotten "under his skin," and what had begun as a therapeutic enterprise was now "an affair of the heart."

3. *Visual imagery.* In translating a thought into a visual image, transformations in the thought are to be expected. Abstractions become concretized; connections disappear; the past and future tenses become present tense; conditional and subjunctive modes become indicative. Like a cartoon illustration, only certain features are illustrated or exaggerated, and others are omitted. The result is often unexpectedly creative and vivid. For example, in the course of his psychoanalysis, a man had become increasingly concerned about the way in which he was, as he verbalized it, "drifting through life" and "coasting along" on his previous accomplishments. On a night following a psychoanalytic interview during which he first cautiously confronted his tendency to "coast along," he dreamed that he was effortlessly sailing down the *coast*-line of the United States—"coasting down the coast," as he put it. Freud saw in this process a reversion to an early, archaic mode of thinking; for early in ontogenetic development, thinking proceeded principally without words and was presumed to be based mainly on sensory and motor imagery. Freud assumed that the sensory impressions of earliest thinking were stored and arranged as memory schemata. Only later in development were words attached to these impressions. The dream work, in submitting thoughts to sensory transformations, offered the thoughts to a regressive course and transformed them into forms more like these earlier, nonverbal, sensory and motor modes.

4. *Secondary revision.* The final characteristic of the dream work, secondary revision, imparts continuity and synthesis to the disparate sensory images. The individual dream elements are probably disconnected and discontinuous with each other, for the entire dream is not a carefully constructed story but a series of thoughts in sensory form. The fourth feature of the dream work is the arrangement of these sensory elements into a coherent structure. In the course of this final arrangement there are additions and deletions with new shifts of accent. Much of the dream's incoherence and internal contradictoriness and illogicality fades, thus imparting a further transformation and disguise of the latent dream thoughts, in the service of which the latent thoughts may undergo further transformation and distortion.

THE YIELD OF DREAMS

Thus, by applying the method of free association to the content of dreams, Freud discovered the phenomenon of distortion. Examination of children's dreams—undertaken in the hope of discovering their meaning because they are so simple and apparently undistorted—revealed the inevitable appearance in dreams of a fulfilled wish. Both adults' and children's dreams disclosed that the essence of dreaming was in the translation of daytime thoughts into sensory images. If one assumed that the daytime thoughts persisted, even though they were not in consciousness at all times, and were a stimulus to be dealt with for the sake of sleep, one could then regard the purpose of the dream work as that of getting rid of the disturbing stimulus. In children's dreams the disturbing stimulus was an unfulfilled wish of the previous day which the dream fulfilled in its hallucinatory activity. Interpretation of adults' dreams showed the same infantile thought modes that appeared in children's dreams. Apparently, then, according to the hypothesis, all dreams—children's and adults'—reflected the same mental mechanism and the presence of wishes and urges.

PUNISHMENT AND ANXIETY DREAMS

Wish fulfillment, or attempted wish fulfillment, is not immediately apparent in several different kinds of dreams, such as dreams with distressing or frightening content, those with attendant anxiety or punishment, or those whose accompanying affect is pleasurable but whose content is either innocuous or clearly undesirable. In each of these cases Freud was able to show by argument and by illustration that they are consistent with the hypothesis of wish fulfillment. These demonstrations, of course, are not proofs but logical disputation. In the frightening anxiety or punishment dream, Freud reasoned that the content was a fulfilled wish that was unacceptable to one aspect of the dreamer's value system.

In the case of punishment and anxiety dreams, Freud assumed that the dreamer was depicted as being divided against himself: one aspect of himself wished for something that another aspect of himself despised. This same intrapersonal conflict was to be seen in his formulations about neurosis. Although he never took seriously the concretization of these aspects of self which seemed to war with each other, he did attempt several ways of conceptualizing them and of giving them a place in general theory. Always he saw one aspect as representing drives and the other as representing controlling structures and purposes. Therefore, in his study of dreams with painful content or affect where the wish fulfillment is obscure, he tried to determine which aspect of the person was having its wish fulfilled. Freud never maintained that wishes were the only thoughts to be uncovered in dreams. Intentions, reminiscences, warnings, reflections, and so on, all could be part of the latent content of dreams. Wishes were different in that they were the thoughts which motivate the dream; other thoughts appeared more as "hangers-on" or incidentals.

> A dream may . . . be any sort of thing insofar as you are only taking into account the thoughts it represents—a warning, an intention, the preparation and so on; but it is always also the fulfillment of an unconscious wish and, if you are considering it as a product of the dream work, it is only that. A dream is therefore never simply an intention, or a warning, but always an intention, etc., translated into the archaic mode of thought by the help of an unconscious wish and transformed to fulfill that wish. The one characteristic, the wish fulfillment, is the invariable one; the other may vary. It may for its part once more be a wish, in which case the dream will, with the help of an unconscious wish, represent as fulfilled the latent wish of the previous day [Freud, 1916–1917, p. 224].

In the close investigation of the thought processes appearing in dreams, Freud began the study of thought and thinking that has its continuation today in the work of Piaget (1952) and Werner (1948) and their students. The developmental aspects of thinking, the rudimentary forms of later logical thought, the persistence into adult life of infantile thought modes were all subjected to examination and description by Freud. He did more than scrutinize only the formal aspects of thinking. He studied the content also: a range of desires, wishes, and urges felt by adults to be both valuable and appalling. These wishes, unacceptable to consciousness during the day but active at night through the entrance of the dream into consciousness, became the nub of an enormously complex model of the psychic apparatus and of several theories of mental functioning. We will now discuss several of these in the chapter that follows.

Summary

Freud became skeptical of the literal truth of many of his patients' reports of early traumatic sexual experiences, yet their persistence puzzled him. He assumed that they represented fantasies which themselves reflected sexual motivations present in early childhood. Thus, the search for actual precipitating causes of neuroses was replaced by a scrutiny of his patients' sexual motivations from early childhood on, a history that included constitutional and experiential factors, as well as elaborations of fantasy. The further development of a number of psychoanalytic formulations was based on studies of everyday "symptom" behavior such as slips of the tongue and dreams. In these phenomena, as in neurotic symptoms, Freud discovered common elements of conflict between a wish and a counterwish; the dream or error represented a compromise between both sides of the conflict. Thus, the principle of continuity between normal and pathological behavior was firmly established within psychoanalysis. Further examination of these everyday psychopathological phenomena led Freud to distinguish the illogical and distorted thinking characteristic of dreams from the logical thinking characteristic of the waking life of most adults. He assumed that the former kind of thinking was typically used to disguise the latent dream wishes. Freud thus postulated a censorship process which functioned to prevent the latent wishes from entering the dream in clear form.

CHAPTER 7

THE MODEL OF THE MIND

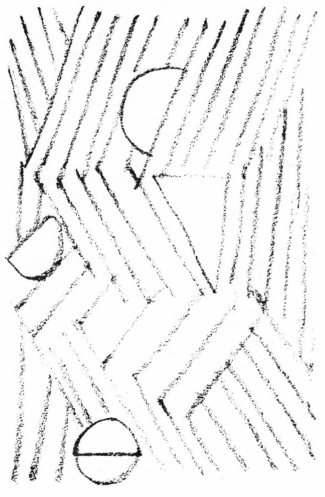

Having detailed his theory that dreams have meaning in terms of the dreamer's purposes, Freud next constructed a model of the mental apparatus that provided for the occurrence of dreams and for the kind of thinking characteristic of them. This model, however, had to be general enough to include mental activities, not only of sleep, but also of waking. This construction is the cornerstone of psychoanalytic psychology. It included explanations of a number of psychological acts such as perception, attention, and memory; it examined forms of thinking from the logical to the primitive; it contained a theory of consciousness and of repression which dealt with the motivated removal of ideas from consciousness. Although the outline of the theory is set forth in chapter VII of *The Interpretation of Dreams* and was elaborated and modified in many subsequent papers, this theoretical system was first advanced several years earlier. In 1895 Freud had, in the space of a few weeks, outlined a *neurological* theory of the mind that bears a close similarity to his later psychological theory. He never published his neurological speculations—his "Psychology for Neurologists," as he referred to it, or the "Project for a Scientific Psychology," as it is referred to today (1895c)—for he quickly became dissatisfied with his attempts to explain psychological phenomena on the basis of neuronal functioning. Even today many psychologists agree with Freud's judgment about the methodological dangers of such reductionism. Yet his attempt is worth noticing because it contains many psychological insights, not the least of which is his premise that *psychopathology can be understood only with reference to normal psychology*. In this respect, he wrote about "The Project" in a letter to his friend, Wilhelm Fliess, on May 25, 1895:

> I am plagued with two ambitions: to see how the theory of mental functioning takes shape if quantitative considerations, a sort of economics of nerve-force, are introduced into it; and secondly, to extract from psychopathology what may be of benefit to normal psychology. Actually a satisfactory general theory of neuropsychotic disturbances is impossible if it cannot be brought into association with clear assumptions about normal mental processes [1887–1902, pp. 119–120].

The *Project for a Scientific Psychology* is tersely written, and since Freud never seriously considered publishing it, it lacks his characteristic lucidity. Highly abstract ideas were advanced in condensed formulations. It is worth exploring some of the main features of "The Project," however, not only to grasp the ingenuity of many of his ideas, but to appreciate the extraordinary power of Freud's reasoning. An appreciation of "The Project" in all its complexities, however, is not necessary for an understanding of the major lines of psychoanalytic theory. Therefore, should the neurological theorizing appear distracting to the reader, he may skip this section and proceed to the discussion of the mental apparatus which begins on page 85.

"The Project"

THE NEURONIC MODEL

Freud first presented two general ideas: (1) activity and rest are distinguished from each other by quantitative considerations and (2) the physical laws of motion govern whatever quantities are involved. The quantitative approach and the belief that mental processes have a neurological substrate subject to physical and biological laws underlie this entire effort of theory construction.

The quantitative approach rests on the clinical observation that excessively intense ideas, such as those occurring in obsessional and hysterical conditions, press peremptorily for action and resolution. For example, a patient may feel strongly compelled to check the gas outlets in spite of knowing that not 5 minutes before he turned them off. Observations such as these suggested to Freud that ideas have a quantitative dimension (magnitude) as well as a qualitative one. He elaborated this conception into a physicalistic theory of how the mind handles such quantities. He conceived the notion that all mental functioning obeys "the principle of neuronic inertia," namely, that the nervous system and individual neurons, like all physical objects, tend to remain at rest unless pushed by another force. If disturbed by an outside force, the system will attempt to rid itself of the disturbance and return to its original resting state. This concept is an early formulation of what later became known as *the pleasure principle,* a basic regulating principle of the organism hypothesized by Freud.

The principle of neuronic inertia, according to Freud, has its evolutionary consequences in the anatomical division of the nervous system into sensory and motor fibers. A neuron, having been excited or, in

Freud's language, having received a quantity, tries to get rid of it through connecting pathways to the motor system. The quantity of excitation which enters the neuronic system provides the source of power for the motor system. A number of different motor pathways are open for this discharge. For example, pathways to the limbs may be chosen to execute flight or simple withdrawal from the source of the excitation. The paths which previously have discharged quantities successfully are more likely to be taken subsequently.

The task of ridding the system of quantities of excitation is complicated, however, by the fact that the nervous system receives stimuli not only from external sources but from within the organism as well, as in hunger. Because the organism cannot withdraw from these inner stimuli, it, therefore, cannot employ their quantity for flight. These stimuli will cease only if certain conditions in the external world are fulfilled—for example, if nourishment is obtained. Thus, survival requires the organism to tolerate or retain a quantity of excitation that is sufficient to produce purposeful action to remove the stimuli—an action that surely requires not a reflex withdrawal (which in the case of internal stimulation is not possible) but a purposeful environmental manipulation. Thus the exigencies of internal stimuli require the organism to supersede temporarily the tendency to reduce stimuli to zero. But delay of discharge thus imposed does not abrogate the basic regulation by the principle of neuronic inertia.

These theoretical postulates find their way into later psychoanalytic theory through several constructs: wish fulfillment (the experience of need reduction by a desired need-satisfying object), the pleasure principle (direct reduction of tension), and the reality principle (reduction of tension through delayed reality-adapted behavior).

The neuronic model imposes a task of reconciling the quantitative theory with the theory of the nervous system as it existed at the turn of the century. In that theory, each neuron is in contact with the neuron that precedes it in the chain through branchlike end-structures called *dendrites,* a special kind of receptor structure. A neuron receives a quantity of excitation from the preceding neuron through its dendrites and transmits it along its long cell-process, the *axon.* For this transmission to occur, the neuron must be in a special state: it must be filled with a certain amount of excitation; an "empty" neuron, when stimulated, can transmit nothing. This hypothetical state of a neuron being filled by a quantity in order for transmission of that quantity to occur is like that of a wire that transmits an electric current. An electron entering the wire cannot cause a current to flow unless the wire is already filled with electrons; it is those electrons already in the wire that are forced out by the entering electrons.

Freud referred to the neuron's state of being filled with this unspecified quantity of excitation as *Bezetzung*. In German this was a familiar, nontechnical word meaning simply "occupation," as when an army occupies a town. Although the term has been translated into the unfamiliar and technical term "cathexis" (borrowed from the Greek), it was really the familiar, graphic meaning that Freud intended to convey. In the language of neuroanatomy, the principle of neuronic inertia is expressed by the hypothesis that in a filled or "cathected" neuron, a quantity of current passes from the reception (dendrite) end of a neuron, past its cell body, and onward along its axon to the point of contact with the next neuron. Each neuron is, therefore, a model in miniature of the entire nervous system, the dendrites serving as the sensory, and the axon the motor, portion.

Neuronal energy or "quantity" can be conceived in terms of being stored or contained within the neuron if one postulates that there are resistances that oppose discharge. Such resistances or barriers would, of course, be found at the points of contact between the neurons. Thus, in 1895 Freud predicted the existence of something corresponding to the actual anatomical synapses between neurons—structures which were discovered in 1897 by Sir Charles Sherrington.

PERCEPTION AND MEMORY

To explain the fact that paths of discharge are established selectively and that only those paths that prove themselves efficient as discharge channels are retained, Freud had to construct a theory of "neuronal memory." Freud developed such a theory by postulating that after excitation, some nervous elements were permanently altered while others returned, unaltered, to their preexcitation state. Those whose alteration had been only temporary, even fleeting, would, upon recovery, again be open to receive new excitations just as they had before. Thus, two classes of neurons were postulated: receptive neurons, whose momentary physiological changes are rapidly erased, and retentive neurons, whose structural changes are permanent and thus reflect memory traces. Freud's closely reasoned argument, then, established a relationship between memory and enduring patterns of neuronal structures, on the one hand, and between perception and fleeting ones on the other.

Neuronal perceptual pathways must remain unaltered by the stimuli they receive in order to be receptive to new incoming stimuli. Memory —the storage of perceptual experiences for later retrieval—must consist in alterations in the configurations of neuronal pathways. Freud's deductive reasoning, therefore, required one to assume that in a model of the mind's workings, memory and perception must be relegated to separate systems.

Given such a neuronal structure, Freud postulated that the psychic apparatus functioned as follows: a quantity of excitation impinges on a sense organ which, through its screening function, transmits only a small quantity of that stimulation. This reduced stimulus excites the trend of the nervous system toward discharge via one of the routes previously facilitated; that is, discharge (action and behavior) is not a random or reflex response to the stimulus but is directed and steered on the basis of prior experience. In this scheme, a concept of motivation provides direction and selection of chosen discharge pathways and is interwoven with perception, memory, and learning.

CONSCIOUSNESS

Freud next considered the question of how consciousness arises. In the model, memory was considered as a system of structures without regard to whether such memories were conscious. Consciousness, he argued, was a property which gave the organism qualitative information about changes occurring within the organism and in the outer world. Whether an idea was in or out of consciousness did not depend upon any inherent properties of the physical stimuli. Rather it resulted from something inherent in the *receptors* of the organism. But consciousness could not be identified either with the perceptual neurons—for many incoming sensations do not have the quality of consciousness—or with those involved with the storage of memories—for only periodically does one become aware of certain memories. Consciousness thus had to be the product of yet a third system of neurons, one separate from perception and from memory. Like the neurons involved in the receiving of sensations, the neurons involved in consciousness played no role in the storage of these phenomena. Thus, consciousness was added to memory and perception in separate neuronal systems.

In the neuronic model, consciousness is a threshold phenomenon. Stimuli have to attain a certain intensity in order to excite the neuronal system responsible for consciousness. For example, stimuli which arise from the center of the organism, "endogenous stimuli" like hunger or sexual arousal, arise continuously. Only periodically, however, do they become manifest as psychological stimuli. Their level of intensity, or their "quantity," must accumulate until it reaches a threshold, at which point psychological awareness can occur. Since the intensity of stimuli varies, some stimuli do not always attain this threshold level.

PAIN

In his later theorizing, Freud assigned a key role to the experience of pain in its physical and psychological forms (for example, as anxiety, q.v. page 140). In his early neurological model in "The Project," he developed a theory of how pain is central to the development of a child's relationship to people.

Freud conceived of pain as the organism's experience of heightened stimulation. The more the cumulative rise in stimulation, the greater the pain. If the pain results from external stimulation, the organism can find relief by removing itself from the offending source; but withdrawal from internally arising stimuli is not possible. Thus the strain caused by unpleasant endogenous stimulation requires a different solution than withdrawal; complex actions are required, and some are more effective than others. A principal method is motor expression, such as crying; although such behavior does not result in direct relief of pain, it usually does succeed in bringing the organism into contact with people who can change the environment in such a way as to bring relief—for example, the hungry infant is fed. The immature organism will thus tend to perceive people in the environment, especially caretakers, primarily in terms of their role as tension-relievers: they come to the infant, minister to him, and provide relief from the distress of excessive stimulation.

Relations with people are, thus, in large measure initiated by the organism's need to escape from pain. Only secondarily do these people take on importance in their own right. The motor behavior that was at first only an expression of pain due to the heightened stimulation by unmet needs or drives (crying when hungry, for example) later takes on a social and communicative function; for the cessation of the hunger experience is coupled with social relationships with the mother. In Freud's words, "In this way the path of discharge [the vocal expression in crying] acquires a secondary function of the highest importance, that of communication [1895 c, p. 318]."

THE EGO

Thus Freud considered that the source of all motives other than the primal ones arose from the infant's helplessness in the face of his needs and drives. Affection for the mother and a variety of wishes (q.v. page 96) were attributed to the effects of previous pleasurable states derived from having one's needs met and one's tensions relieved. However, because the infant does not remain totally dependent upon caretaking people for the rest of his life, one must postulate that there is a slowly developed network of pathways which enables the infant to take an active part in finding satisfaction and in relating himself to people who can help to provide such satisfaction. This network was considered by Freud to be part of an executive or organizing function of the organism that arose from the capacity of the system to delay immediate discharge and to store excitation. Freud referred to this set of organizing functions as the *ego*.

In addition to those sketched above, many profound ideas are to be found in "The Project," some of which have never been developed beyond their mere statement. There are interesting speculations by Freud on the differences between reproductive and critical thought, remembering, judgment, will, attention, and speech mechanisms. It is clear that a preliminary schema of what the structure of the mind must be like was formulated by Freud by 1895. But the difficulties of constructing a consistent theory and mental model in neurological terms proved too formidable. Many psychological phenomena defied reduction or translation to such terms. Freud thus abandoned the plan of "The Project" and never published the work. Many of the ideas of mental functioning that he developed in "The Project" still seemed sound to him, even without the neurological scaffolding. Within a few years he made a new and more psychological effort to construct a model of the mind, but one which preserved a number of the ideas from "The Project." This new attempt stemmed from his consideration of dreams and appears in the final chapter of *The Interpretation of Dreams*.

A Model of the Mind

We have already noted that just as anatomists and physiologists constructed theories of normal structure and function from illness, disease, and morbidity, so Freud's observations of neurotic phenomena generated speculations about normal psychological functioning. Freud used this procedure most skillfully in his consideration of dreams. His neurotic patients frequently told him their dreams, and in his own self-psychoanalysis, Freud scrutinized his own dreams. Thus it seemed reasonable to begin the construction of a model of the mind with the consideration of the dreams as a psychological phenomenon. For surely any model of the mind that claims completeness would have to encompass not only the rational waking functions, but also the strange thought formations typical of dream states.

To construct a model of the mind and to formulate a number of hypotheses about its functioning are at best uncertain undertakings. Freud was aware of the methodological pitfalls of any ad hoc theory conceived to fit only a single set of data—like those provided by dreams or by neuroses.

> No conclusions upon the construction and working methods of the mental instrument can be arrived at or at least fully proved from even the most painstaking investigation of dreams or of any other mental function taken in isolation. To achieve this result it will be necessary to correlate all the established implications derived from a comparative study of a whole series of such functions. Thus, the psychological hypotheses to which we are led by an analysis of the processes of dreaming must be left, as it were, in suspense until they can be related to the findings of other inquiries which seek to approach the kernel of the same problem from another angle [Freud, 1900, p. 511].

The other angle he alluded to here was the study of psychopathology. Hypotheses about the psychic apparatus and models derived from investigations of dreams and of psychopathology, he insisted, had to be consistent with each other.

Before Freud discussed the phenomenon of dreaming, he addressed himself to the adequacy of the dream as a datum. How can one discuss dreams when the dream is known to us only through the dreamer's report, especially when the dreamer often may not know if the dream occurred? In his clinical work, Freud had noted that important parts of dreams were forgotten or distorted. In interpreting dreams in the context of his treatment of patients, Freud had accepted those distortions and omissions as important parts of the dream narrative and yet had been able to arrive at sensible and helpful interpretations. His successful interpretative method gave equal attention to all aspects of the dream report, including fragments and distortions as if the data were indeed adequate. There is, however, a theoretical justification, which outweighs the empirical one, for Freud's practice of proceeding as if a dream report were a valid reflection of the actual dream. Freud thought that the process of forgetting and elaborating the dream was not an arbitrary event but was determined like any other piece of behavior and thought. The forgetting of dreams, doubts about the elements of a dream, indistinctness of details in dreams, and revisions in the retelling of dreams could be regarded as reflections of dream censorship. Since they were thus an integral part of the dream *narration*, they had to be taken into account no less than the hypothetical dream as it actually had occurred. Freud saw these elements as deriving from a process of resisting the emergence into consciousness of dream thoughts rather than from any mutually alien states of waking and sleeping. He noted that a dream interpreted in the waking state may be suddenly forgotten and with it the interpretation which was, from its inception, a product of the waking state.

In the face of resistance against the dream thoughts entering consciousness, then, how did dreams come about at all? Freud's tentative answer was that during sleep a dream was possible because the strength of the censorship had somehow been reduced or circumvented. The dream, he reasoned, could not have come about if the censorship remained as intense or as consistent at night as it was during the day. But this was a provisional answer and one that Freud used only as a starting point and subsequently modified in the course of his progressive examination of the mental apparatus.

Before proceeding with his construction, Freud dealt further with the use of the patient's free associations as primary data for unraveling the meaning of dreams of whose existence the patient was no longer aware. Freud anticipated a host of objections to his technique of allowing the patient's thoughts to ramble freely, on the basis of elements of the dream, and assuming that what emerged could be accepted as the dream's meaning. He realized that the critics would argue that what he considered to be the common thread of meaning running through the dream might be an artifact of his technique. Was is not possible that by chance a common theme might be found among disparate elements or a theme once identified in the course of associations might influence the content of subsequent thoughts without having truly been part of the dream at all?

Freud gave both empirical and theoretical answers to these objections. Empirically he pointed out that when a similar technique had been used to unravel the meaning of some neurotic symptoms, it had been fruitful as shown by the disappearance of the symptoms. If, as Freud assumed, the dream had a structure similar to that of a neurotic symptom, the technique might be similarly valid as a way to ferret out its meaning. The theoretical answer that he gave, however, is the more persuasive one. Associations, he said, were not arbitrary. While we might be able to ignore or overcome directing ideas that were conscious, it is not possible for us to obliterate nonconscious determining tendencies and sets. Indeed, thinking often proceeds principally with ideas whose organization and direction are not freely available to consciousness. In some psychopathological conditions, such as delirium, and even in milder forms of illness, such as neurosis, peculiar associations may occur. These associations may appear to be arbitrary, but in fact they are not. One can demonstrate that more meaningful connections have been replaced by arbitrary ones, and this replacement is brought about by the pressure of the censorship. Freud thus formulated two general statements about thought processes: (1) When conscious purposive thoughts are abandoned, concealed purposive ideas assume control of the current of ideas; and (2) superficial associations are only substituted, by displacement, for suppressed deeper ones. Thus, by the process of free association and by abandoning conscious purposive ideas, one permits unknown ideas to direct the associations thus leading to the meaning of the dream.

THE SIX FACTORS OF DREAMS

To continue the chronology, Freud now turned to the task of constructing a model of the psychic apparatus. He had already prepared his readers for this task by arguing that the dream as a *thought*—as opposed to a somatic phenomenon—had six factors: (1) Dreams are psychological acts with meaning; (2) they are motivated by a wish which has not yet been fulfilled; (3) the wish is not consciously recognized and appears only in distorted form because of the censorship; (4) the dream may exhibit elements which are actually a condensation of several different things; (5) material is presented in sensory images; (6) there is a tendency to make the dream a rational and intelligible product. Freud set himself the task of exploring the relationship among these factors, particularly between the dream as a wishful psychological act and four of the other factors: the censorship, the peculiar thought products, the sensory hallucinatory quality, and the regard for intelligibility. A model of the psychic apparatus had to be constructed that would include these factors and their relationships.

THE SENSORY VIVIDNESS OF DREAMS

The essential feature of dreams is their hallucinatory quality. A model of the mind had to provide for the production of such vivid hallucinatory experiences. To understand this feature of dreams, Freud referred to a rather obscure statement of G. T. Fechner's that "the scene of action in dreams is different from that of waking ideational life [Freud, 1900, p. 536]." According to Fechner, the dream thus takes place almost literally in another world. This concept of psychic localization—as distinguished from anatomical localization—is the pivot of the model. Freud used spatial and quasi-anatomical metaphors purely for heuristic purposes, well aware that the functions he was describing may be separated by time, not space. Even within chapter VII of *The Interpretation of Dreams,* he replaced the topographic model with a model based on energy dynamics. Although the use of models had been widespread in scientific explanation, particularly in preliminary expositions, Freud was quite clear that employing models was a speculation to be used cautiously.

> We are justified, in my view, in giving free rein to our speculations so long as we retain the coolness of our judgment and do not mistake the scaffolding for the building. And since at our first approach to something unknown all that we need is the assistance of provisional ideas, I shall give preference in the first instance to hypotheses of the crudest and most concrete description [Freud, 1900, p. 536].

He asked the reader to consider the mind as an optical instrument, the components of which, like lenses, perform certain functions in the forming of ideas and thoughts. In some parts of the apparatus, the image is virtual or potential. The image becomes actual and real only when it enters a specific component of the psychic system—later to be identified as consciousness.

In continuing his construction of a mental apparatus that would allow for the hallucinatory experience of dreams—as well as for their other features and eventually for psychopathological phenomena—Freud distinguished three characteristics of the apparatus: (1) Stimuli flow through the psychic apparatus generally in one direction; (2) the psychic apparatus is not unitary, but it consists of parts with specific functions; (3) consciousness is an essential feature of the apparatus.

1. The psychic apparatus has a *direction*. Stimuli, whether they arise externally or internally, proceed from the sensory end to the motor end. At the sensory end, stimuli are received as percepts and advance through the apparatus to the motor end where channels of action dispose of the stimulation. Thus the basic structure is that of a reflex system.

2. The psychic apparatus is differentiated, and the agencies at the sensory end have specialized functions concerned with perception. The perceptual apparatus receives stimuli, but it cannot retain them. Retention of stimuli implies a change in the state of the structure that is storing them, and because the perceptual apparatus must remain generally unchanged to receive new impressions, it must be separate from a memory storage system. Perception does, however, provide a sensory quality for the incoming stimuli. A special memory system, however, receives the sensory impressions from the perceptual ap-

paratus and stores them in one of many possible arrangements—for example, filing them according to the principles of association or of conceptual connections. The essence of the theory of memory set forth is that the traces of the incoming stimulus are stored in arrangements that reflect the dynamic and protean meanings of the memories. Memory in this scheme is not a photographic reproduction of the prior perceptual experiences. The traces are stored, but they are recalled by a process of *reconstruction* of the perceptual experiences but without sensory quality. For example, when one hears a story, one can reconstruct its essence but rarely the exact words that were heard. And, after some time, the core of the story-line may undergo changes, with either new elements appearing in it or old ones dropping out.

3. A third characteristic of the apparatus is that it includes the system called consciousness (*Cs*) which is placed at the motor end of the apparatus. Like perception, consciousness contains no permanent records. Sensory qualities are delivered to consciousness by the perceptual system and memories, too, are delivered to consciousness. Memories, of course, can exist and not be in awareness; indeed the vicissitudes and rearrangements of memories occur without consciousness. Thus the functions of memory and of consciousness are different, although related. Freud postulated that the earliest memories laid down before the child had learned to use words were organized according to sensorimotor schemata. Because of this organization, these memories, when revived, have a hallucinatory or perceptual quality. The older the memories, the more this is likely to be true.

THE CENSORSHIP

Completing this bare model of the psychic apparatus is the censorship function. Freud noted how prominent self-criticism is in waking life, and he thus placed the system which directed censorship close to the motor end of the apparatus.

THE PRECONSCIOUS

The final system, the preconscious (*Pcs*) is also placed at the motor end. The term *preconscious* in this model refers both to the location of ideas which have relatively easy access to consciousness and to a system with certain psychological functions. Insofar as its usage as a location of ideas is concerned, Freud attempted to differentiate two kinds of unconscious ideas: (1) There are ideas which, though momentarily out of awareness, can, with minimum effort, be made conscious. One's telephone number or the name of a close friend are examples of such ideas which are descriptively unconscious until they are recalled to consciousness by a small bit of effort. (2) But there are other ideas outside of awareness which defy such efforts at recall and do not easily achieve consciousness. It is as if these ideas are *withheld* from achieving consciousness by some repressing force. Such ideas Freud referred to as *dynamically* unconscious. The term *preconscious ideas* applies to the location of those *descriptively unconscious* ideas whose access to consciousness is relatively easy.

But the term preconscious in the model we are studying also refers to a system with certain properties or functions, such as that of attention, motor activities, certain thought processes like anticipation, concept formation, and concentration; in short, the term refers to many of the functions which Freud 23 years later (1923) subsumed under the term *ego*. In its usage as a system, Freud adopted the abbreviation *Pcs* for the preconscious. We will be discussing its usage as a system at greater length later in this chapter.

Figure 1 shows the model thus constructed—the sensory and motor ends, the separation of perceptual and memory systems, the precon-

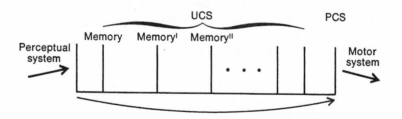

Figure 1 *Freud's spatial model of the mind. Stimuli enter the apparatus at the perceptual end. They are then stored as memories in the memory system, where they become integrated with other memory structures. The stimuli can continue to travel in a forward direction to the motor system, provided there is no impeding force, such as the force of censorship. At the system preconscious (Pcs) they can either again become conscious—by the addition of "attention cathexis"—or be "discharged" in the form of some motor behavior.*

scious system at the motor end, and the bulk of memories designated as dynamically unconscious. Consciousness is not shown in this model.

THE FUNCTIONING OF THE APPARATUS

An excitation that reaches the apparatus is received at the sensory end and becomes a percept. As soon as the excitation ceases, its effects are stored in the memory system.

There are three ways in which an excitation may attain consciousness: (1) If the excitation is of sufficient intensity, part of it can continue its journey to the motor end of the *Pcs* and become conscious; (2) if, however, the stimulation is too weak to attain consciousness on its own, it can attain consciousness by receiving from the *Pcs* an added intensity called *hypercathexis* or *attention cathexis*; (3) a memory which is stored in the unconscious memory system can, like an external stimulus, also traverse the mental apparatus and proceed to the system preconscious. It, too, can become conscious only if a sufficient charge of energy is present, either intrinsically or added from the *Pcs* in the form of attention cathexis.

THE MODEL APPLIED TO DREAMS: REGRESSION

Dreams, then, are formed as follows: Dream thoughts, like other thoughts, must move from the *Ucs* to the *Pcs* to find motor expression or to become conscious. Because dream thoughts represent unwelcome wishes, this path is blocked during the day by the censorship. At night the conditions are altered because the censorship is somewhat relaxed. But it is not just a matter of the relaxation of the censorship at night that produces dreams. If it were, dreams would be like other thoughts; they would be without sensory quality. The sensory, hallucinatory quality of dreams can be explained only by assuming that rather than traveling in the usual direction toward the *Pcs*—the direction shown by the arrows in Figure 1—the dream thoughts follow a *regressive* course back toward the perceptual end of the apparatus. Although relaxed compared to its daytime vigilance, the censorship would still be active and operative; thus the censorship was conceived of as the prime mover of this reversal of excitation.

The reversal is also aided by the fact that during sleep there is a simultaneous raising of sensory thresholds and a diminution of sensory input. The forward progressive flow of sensations is thus considerably reduced. What Freud called the *regression* of the dream thoughts involved three aspects: (1) a topographic regression from the memory systems to the perceptual systems of the hypothetical spatial model; (2) a temporal regression from newer to older memories and other psychological formations, for older memories are more sensory and less verbal in nature; and (3) a formal regression from more advanced to more primitive modes of expression, for the structure of earlier memories was assumed to be less logical than that of more recent ones. These three kinds of regression are three different views of the same process.

TYPES OF WISHES

Freud then examined the phenomenon of wish fulfillment which he had alleged to be the motivational source of all dreams. He described four kinds of wishes, all of which may appear in dreams:

1.   Wishes excited during the day by chance occurrences which, because of circumstances, could not be satisfied—for example, one may have had the wish to attend a particular athletic event, but because of poor weather, the contest was cancelled. Such wishes may easily be recalled to conscious with only mild effort; Freud therefore "located" them in the *Pcs*.

2.   Wishes which during the day had been driven out of the preconscious system into the unconscious because they were unacceptable —for example, hostile wishes toward a good friend.

3.   Wishes that had no relation to daily life but which were linked with unconscious wishes long since expelled from the *Pcs*. For example, a wish to become more powerful than one's father may have been pushed out of the *Pcs* many years ago because the idea of defeating one's own father in aggressive competition may have produced too many feelings of guilt. Such wishes may become active at night, but because of the resistance exerted by the censorship, they are not able to enter the preconscious and thence to become conscious.

4.   Somatic needs which give rise to psychological wishes, such as the wish to quench one's thirst or to satisfy sexual desire.

Although each of these four kinds of wishes may appear in the dream, and each, because of its intensity, might be thought equally effective in producing a dream, Freud argued that only those wishes arising from unconscious sources can be considered as the ultimate instigators of dreams. In adults all the other kinds of wishes have been attenuated into relatively weakened forms by intellectualization, rationalization, and other results of thought structures. Only childhood wishes, which have been previously repudiated but which are stored in the unconscious memory system, retain their intensity. They alone have the force to reverse the current of the psychic apparatus and direct it toward perception. Thus, here again we find the assumption that unconscious impulses are not dead, although they may be temporarily inactive: the unconscious wishes which stimulate dreams are wishes which have never been forgotten and which reach back into the early childhood of the dreamer. This formulation presumes a store of memories that has not been subjected to the transformations of forgetting but which, although not available to consciousness, is nevertheless preserved with astonishing intensity. Research by Penfield and Roberts (1959) has tended to confirm this view of memory and its relations with the perceptual system.

During a brain operation that he was performing to relieve disabling attacks of temporal lobe epilepsy, Penfield in 1938 reported that when he stimulated with low electric current the temporal lobe of his patient who was fully conscious but under a local analgesia, she reexperienced with astonishing vividness an event that occurred during her early childhood. She reported that she even felt the same terror that had accompanied the original episode. Penfield later wrote that in 190 cases which he studied, stimulation of the temporal lobes by mild current produced hallucinations which were extraordinarily congruent with memories of the patients' past lives. All the patients reported that the experience was more vivid than anything they could remember through voluntary effort.

When electrical stimulation recalls the past, the patient has what some of them have called a "flashback." He seems to relive some previous period of time and is aware of those things of which he was conscious in that previous period. . . . Take as an example the words of M. Ma. during stimulation of her right temporal lobe. When . . . a gentle current was switched on, she exclaimed: "Oh, a familiar memory—in an office somewhere. I could see the desks. I was there and someone was calling to me—a man leaning on a desk with a pencil in his hand."

All the detail of those things to which he had paid attention in some previous period of time was still there. Perhaps the pencil in his hand had seemed important, but other images that must have reached her retina during the original experience are now lost, probably because they were ignored originally [Penfield & Roberts, 1959, p. 45].

Thus the model of a regressive stimulation of the perceptual apparatus by old, but preserved, memory processes that have been activated finds some experimental support.

THE DAY RESIDUES

During sleep the thoughts of waking life are placed aside. To the extent that we are able to suspend preconscious thought activity, we can sleep restfully, for successful sleep requires that we reduce to a minimum the activity of preconscious thinking. But there are thoughts that persist into sleep which Freud called *residues of the previous day.* He listed five kinds of such day residues:

1. Tasks left incomplete because of an interruption
2. Tasks left incomplete because of inability or failure
3. Suppressed acts and thoughts
4. Unconscious thoughts which have been stimulated by preconscious thoughts
5. Indifferent incidental impressions

Some of these day residues have the form of preconscious wishes. By themselves these day residues cannot become conscious during sleep, and, therefore, for them to appear in a dream, they must become connected with an unconscious wish which has the force to move in the regressive direction toward perception. The day residue itself lacks the "force" to produce a dream, and the unconscious infantile wishes lack the psychological *content* and representability to appear in a dream, because they are sensorimotor in form and thus quite alienated from contemporary experiences. Freud compared the situation with that of a capitalist and entrepreneur; the former provides the power, and the latter provides the form of the enterprise. The day residues and the infantile wishes must, therefore, amalgamate to become a dream. Sometimes the preconscious and unconscious wishes coincide or oppose each other, and the dream may consequently be pleasant or unpleasant. But a compromise between the two sources of wishes is the general outcome. This theory of motivation by wishes is not specific for dream phenomena; all psychological acts are assumed to be motivated by wishes. *Therefore, symptoms and behavior disorders, too, are to be regarded as compromises between unconscious and preconscious wishes.*

ANALYSIS OF A WISH

But what is a wish? In defining a wish, Freud returned to the neuropsychological model outlined in "The Project," in which he had defined a wish as a memory either of past need satisfactions or relief from unpleasant tension. Freud used as an example an infant who is hungry—has a need for food—and is fed by his mother, leading to need satisfaction. Later, when the same hunger need arises again, it results in a discharge of part of the "quantity" produced by the heightened need. This is a motor discharge and appears as crying or restlessness. Such a motor discharge which reflects a mounting need tension, Freud called an *affect.* As mentioned on page 83, the affect discharge is later employed principally to summon the mother or other person who had satisfied the need before.

In this model, endogenous stimulation—a need that arises—results in an affect which summons the appearance of a person who can provide a need-satisfying object and thus lead to a cessation of the stimulus. The experience of having the stimulus cease is called an *experience of satisfaction.* This experience of satisfaction is a complex one that includes many sensations and perceptions. According to Freud, the perception of the need-satisfying object—for example, the mother's breast—is not a well-structured, visual, or other specific sensory pattern, but rather an undifferentiated, global, sensorimotor experience involving several sense modalities and the infant's motor responses to them. The infant's early experience is thus not to be regarded as a "blooming, buzzing confusion" described by William James nor as a highly differentiated and structured perceptual patterning.

The theory assumes that the infant strongly associates the memory image of the perception of the mother's breast with the actual experience of need satisfaction. Then, at the next arousal of the need, the infant will experience an impulse to reestablish the perception of the previously successful need-satisfying experience, in the magical expectation that to do so will again establish that previous experience of satisfaction. *It is this impulse to reestablish the previous experience of satisfaction that Freud called a wish.* Even when a need-satisfying object is absent, the impulse to reexperience that object continues and results in a hallucination of the need-satisfying object, as if recreating with perceptual vividness the memory of the satisfaction would be tantamount to achieving fulfillment of the wish in reality. Whether perceptual imagery of a hallucinatory quality actually occurs is open to investigation. Piaget's studies would suggest that reproductive imagery is not to be expected in infants until after the start of the second half of the first year. The scheme postulated by Freud, however, is not one requiring the voluntary reproduction of memory-images but rather a reflex experience involving sensorimotor experiences associated with previous need satisfaction.

AN INHIBITORY SYSTEM

Adaptive requirements alter this primitive process, for hallucinating a need-satisfying object clearly does not result in actual need satisfaction. Real need satisfaction requires that the organism inhibit the primitive tendency to hallucinate and that, instead, it initiate voluntary action through which the need-satisfying object can be sought in the real world. Thus in addition to the first system (a wishful one), a second is postulated whose task it is to inhibit the regression to the hallucination and to use the excitation associated with the wish to search the environment for an object congruent with the memory of the need-satisfying object. Thus, this second system requires more complex thought processes than mere wishing; it requires such processes as anticipation of future needs and decisions about congruence between a need and a potentially satisfying object. Yet this second system and its activities are in the service of the fulfillment of wishes no less than the first. Dreams are examples of the psychic apparatus' primitive, but unadaptive, way of working, a way that has been superseded by the second system.

> What once dominated waking life, while the mind was still young and incompetent, seems now to have been banished into the night—just as the primitive weapons, bows and arrows, that have been abandoned by adult men, turn up once more in the nursery. *Dreaming is a piece of infantile*

mental life that has been superseded. These methods of working on the part of the psychical apparatus, which are normally suppressed in waking hours, become current once more in psychosis and then reveal their incapacity for satisfying our needs in relation to the external world [Freud, 1900, p. 567].

The model thus unifies the psychology of impulses and wishes with that of perception, cognition, action, and inhibition. Drives, urges, and wishes, although not yet specifically identified in Freud's 1900 model, provide the motive force for the mental apparatus. They are conceived of as stimuli arising from within the organism. A controlling, inhibiting, or modulating system (later called the *ego*) is required to adapt the needs, drives, and wishes to the ever-changing world around the organism. Thought, memory, and action are all utilized in the service of assuring eventual drive-satisfaction, and regression to hallucinatory perception is a normal function of the psychic apparatus. It should be emphasized that this model is of the presumed primitive psychical apparatus of the infant and not that of the mature adult. The theory does provide for the later appearance of relative independence of the second system from drives. Under some conditions, however, functions of the second system can again come under the domination of the drives, thus giving rise to neurotic and psychotic behavior. That much of our action and thinking during the day is free of drive encroachment can be attributed to the operation of the inhibitory system. Any condition that increases the intensity of the drives, as, for example, in puberty, or decreases the effectiveness of inhibition while the subject is awake, as in states of fatigue or intoxication, results in pathological behavior in speech, thoughts, actions, and affects.

THE MODEL APPLIED TO NEUROSES

The theory of wish fulfillment, developed from the phenomenon of dreams, had to be tested against the clinical phenomena of the psychoneuroses. One would have to find wishes and their inhibition by a second system ("counterwishes") coinciding in neuroses as they do in dreams. And indeed, in neuroses, too, Freud was able to discover not only unconscious wishes but counterwishes which provided self-punishment by serving as reproaches to one's self for harboring unconscious infantile wishes. The neurotic symptoms could be shown to express both tendencies. Freud gives one example of this:

In one of my women patients . . . hysterical vomiting turned out to be on the one hand the fulfillment of an unconscious phantasy dating from her puberty—of a wish, that is, that she might be continuously pregnant and have innumerable children, then a further wish added later, that she have them by as many men as possible. A powerful defense of impulse had sprung up against this unbridled wish. And since the patient might lose her figure and her good looks as a result of her vomiting, and so might cease to be attractive to anyone, this symptom was acceptable to the punitive train of thought as well; and since it was permitted by both sides it could become a reality [1900, p. 570].

THE WISH FOR SLEEP

Dreams, likewise, may contain not only the unconscious infantile wishes (which are assumed to be the ultimate motivators of the dream) and some ancillary wishes as well, but also several counterwishes originating in the second system, many of which express reality-attuned thoughts. One of these wishes can be identified as a general wish for sleep, a wish that turns away all disturbing stimuli, including those that arise from aroused unconscious infantile wishes. The essential feature of the design thus requires the infantile unconscious wish to arise and seek fulfillment at night because of the reduction both of the censorship and of the flow of exogenous stimulation. But it is countered by a still existent inhibitory system which functions as a preserver of sleep and thus provides an important condition for the regressive flow of the dream thoughts. Freud refers to this as the preconscious wish to sleep.

SUMMARY OF THE MODEL

To recapitulate this rather elaborate scheme, Freud postulated that during sleep the residues of the previous day's thoughts remain in the preconscious system. An unconscious infantile wish links itself with some of the day's residues of experiences in the preconscious and by that linkage acquires a representability. But by the same linkage, the day residues have coupled themselves with the unconscious wish which had previously been barred as unacceptable from the preconscious and from consciousness. Now the day residues and the unconscious infantile wish which they are transporting proceed toward the motor end of the apparatus—to consciousness. They cannot find expression, however, because of the organismic changes that occur during sleep: the motor system is paralyzed and arousal thresholds of the preconscious system are heightened. They are also blocked from further advance by the censorship which objects to the content of the unconscious wish. The wish then begins its regressive course, connecting itself with earlier memories and fantasies which have increasingly visual or other sensory characteristics, until finally it reaches the perceptual end of the apparatus. It then stimulates the perceptual apparatus and, like any other percept, is noticed by consciousness and is then worked over and organized.

CONSCIOUSNESS AND ATTENTION

The statement that the percept "is noticed by consciousness" was further spelled out by Freud. He assumed that for something to become conscious it must depend on drawing or attracting to itself a quantity of an unspecified type of energy, attention (or attention cathexis), which he assumed to be available in limited amounts. Thoughts which failed to attract sufficient attention cathexis were by no means prevented from developing, and indeed Freud felt that they might even enjoy a more luxuriant growth without the focus of attention being on them. Ideas governing conscious thoughts—strivings, attitudes, prejudices, and anticipations, for example—might actually inhibit thought and associations by keeping them logical and attuned to reality. But where no attention cathexis was attached to an idea, where it had been withdrawn from the idea, or where the idea became linked with an unconscious wish, that idea then became subject to transformations which were quite uncharacteristic of normal, logical, everyday conscious thinking. Put another way, when the binding and controlling effects of the attention of consciousness are withdrawn from an idea, and when an unconscious wish then connects with it (transfers its cathexis to it), that idea loses its easy accessibility to the consciousness and becomes transformed in a variety of ways.

THE PRIMARY AND SECONDARY PROCESSES

There are four kinds of transformations that may be undergone by ideas that have lost the controlling attention of consciousness and simultaneously have become linked with unconscious wishes. These have been referred to as *condensation, displacement, illogic,* and the *coexistence of opposites.*

1. *Condensation.* As we previously noted, the manifest dream is always more terse and succinct than the latent dream thoughts, as if many of the former had been condensed into the latter. Free associations to the elements of manifest dreams seem to proliferate and involve many ideas from many different quarters of a person's life. Consider the following short dream by a young woman in psychoanalytic treatment, and note how the terseness of the dream gives way to a host of connected ideas.

The dream: "A man from Forbes came to visit me."

The patient's associations may be paraphrased as follows: Forbes is the name of a USAF base nearby. A plane had crashed there two days ago, killing three crewmen. The patient's analyst was about to leave on a short trip, a fact that angered the patient not only because it would disrupt her treatment but also because it revived memories of the time her father left the family for several months when the patient was five years old. As a little girl, she had fantasied that her father had left because she was naughty, but as time went on, she began to experience anger toward her father, an emotion which was congruent with her mother's feelings—at times openly expressed—about the separation. The patient had entertained ideas that she wished that her analyst would crash in a plane and was frightened by those wishes, a circumstance that echoed the earlier experiences in connection with the separation from her father. The patient's fiancé had been killed in an automobile accident several years ago, and it was her extended brooding over that incident that had urged her to seek treatment for herself. Her own hostility towards the men who kept leaving her was an attitude of which she had not been aware.

The event of the plane crash at Forbes Air Force Base provided a conscious representation in which were condensed many strands of her history of hates and loves. Like condensations in poetry, single words or images can be charged with multiple meanings, only some of which are immediately accessible to consciousness.

2. *Displacement.* Some of the quantitative charge or intensity of an unconscious wish can be displaced onto a preconscious, apparently innocuous, idea, so that the latter gains a prominence that is not warranted by its logical or reality significance. For example, in the patient's dream about the man from Forbes, rather than her dead fiancé, her analyst, or her father, she dreams of an unknown man. Further, there is a *visit* rather than a departure or a death. The day before the dream she actually was visited by a door-to-door salesman, a not uncommon event. This event seemed to prime many associations about visits and reunions, and for some time during the psychoanalytic interview, while she was associating to the dream, she was distracted from the idea of departures, terminations, and deaths, while she was concentrating on reunions and visits. It is not insignificant for this patient that she typically attempted to come to terms with her anger and death wishes by "reversing" them, or turning them into their opposite. In this example, separation, departure, and a death wish are represented by a "visit."

Displacement is a prominent feature of the formation of a phobia which is—in a restricted sense—an intense urge to avoid situations or objects with which anxiety is connected, such as bridges, open or closed spaces, or certain animals. Psychoanalytic investigation has shown that these phobic objects are generally displacements of an original childhood fear—of, say, punishment by a parent—to an innocuous object. Freud demonstrated the role of displacement in the analysis of an agoraphobia—fear of open places—and a horse phobia in a five-year-old boy (Freud, 1909). He showed that the boy, Hans, wanted his mother's exclusive affection and regarded his father as an unwanted rival and therefore also feared him. The agoraphobia served the purpose of keeping Hans close to his mother; the horse phobia allowed Hans to displace his fear of his father onto the horse and thus maintain a relationship with his father.

3. *Illogic.* The connections between the ideas are loose and illogical, based at times on farfetched similarities, puns, and homonyms.

4. *Coexistence of opposites.* Contradictions and opposites may exist alongside each other without compromise and reconciliation.

These thought qualities (and some others which are characteristic of dreams and can also be seen in some psychotic thinking) are called the *primary process.* This way of thinking has an uninhibited quality and seems characteristic of infantile thought.

The secondary process, characteristic of preconscious and consciously directed thinking, is more controlled and controlling. It is typical of later developmental stages of thinking.

Here again there are two systems, one in which activity is directed toward immediate discharge and the other in which activity is directed toward inhibiting and directing that discharge. The second system requires a large storehouse of memories freely at its command in order to direct the organism to an action that, in the long run, satisfies the wish arising in the first system. The first system is identified as the *unconscious* and the second the *preconscious*.

Freud examined the hypothetical psychic apparatus when its function of discharge—wish satisfaction—was not working smoothly. Such a situation arises when an intense stimulus impinges upon it from exogenous or endogenous sources. The heightened intensity of stimulation experienced as pain results in uncoordinated motor movements which continue until the stimulus disappears. Upon a second appearance of the noxious stimulus, the previously successful movement will recur. The organism strives urgently to avoid the painful stimulus. Its flight from perceiving the painful stimulus is the prototype of what in a later, more developed form is the mental mechanism of repression. The first system—the unconscious—is capable only of discharging wishes, and, therefore, it cannot serve the functions of inhibition and avoidance necessary for flight. The second system—the preconscious—performs this function instead by controlling wishes which may be inappropriate, unwelcome, or incompatible either with reality or with the second system's standards of behavior.

As the organism strives to prevent the release of the pain that accompanies the perceiving of an unwelcome wish, the control systems may attempt to substitute a more innocuous wish and its object: for example, anger and aggression at one's employer instead of fury at one's father. To accomplish control through substitution, the preconscious system requires access to as many memories and thoughts as possible—including even those whose perception may momentarily bring pain. Indeed, being able to endure such pain seems necessary for the smooth functioning of the psychic apparatus. Memories, which if they remained in consciousness would bring severe pain, must be recognized—at least for a moment—in order for the preconscious system to inform itself about the nature of those memories and thus be able to deal with them. One cannot avoid something without knowing of its painful existence or consequences. Thus, ultimately, fulfillment of wishes through finding the wished-for object in the world—"identity of perception'—and the avoidance of pain regulate both the unconscious and preconscious systems. Thought, as in the scanning of painful memories in the interest of adaptation, is conceived of as experimental action.

PRIMAL REPRESSION AND SECONDARY REPRESSION

Freud assumed that primary process thinking is characteristic of the very young human being, while only later does the secondary process assume dominance. There are two consequences of this chronology: (1) Wishes emanating from needs and drives early in life tend to remain alien to the more logical thought organization that develops later. The preconscious system acting under the dominance of the reality principle to control action and logical thinking can direct and steer, delay and detour wishful impulses, but it cannot obliterate them. (2) A second consequence of the chronological development of thought processes is that while early unconscious wishes still carry with them archaic sensorimotor qualities, these qualities are inaccessible to the more logical preconscious system. The assumption of the inaccessibility of early memories to the preconscious is called *primal repression*. These primal repressed memories, cut off from any access to consciousness, would doubtless generate pain or anxiety if, by way of their derivatives, they were able to manifest themselves in action or in consciousness. For example, the wish to smear feces, once pleasurable, later produces disgust. The theory maintains that the wish to smear feces actually does not disappear but persists. However, because its sensorimotor form was determined prior to the differentiation of secondary process thinking, it is not accessible to the preconscious system and, therefore, to consciousness. The wish may however link itself, by displacement, with thoughts which *are* available to the preconscious system. Part of the cathexis of the wish to smear may thus become displaced onto previously innocuous preconscious ideas. A wish to touch mud may develop, for example. At this point the preconscious may become aware of the forbidden wish behind this originally innocuous one and may react with a similar revulsion or anxiety to this earlier harmless wish to touch mud. The derivative wish to touch mud may also be made unavailable to consciousness or repressed. Thus *repression proper* (or *secondary* repression, as distinguished from the *primal* repression, which dealt with the early infantile wish to smear feces) consists of rejection from consciousness or from the preconscious of ideas related to already unwelcome unconscious wishes. Note how this formulation is similar to the earlier idea of defense outlined in Chapter 3.

THE RETURN OF THE REPRESSED: IN DREAMS AND NEUROSIS

The repressed unconscious ideas may at one time or another become reinforced by another unconscious wish and with this added "strength" attempt to force their way to the preconscious system and into action. A defensive struggle then takes place, and varied forms of compromise are tried. For example, the wish to play with mud may be permitted under certain conditions, such as when gardening and baking (kneading bread dough) or during artistic pursuits, as in modeling. Or a symptom may develop that expresses a compromise between the repressed wish and the defense: the person may meticulously avoid all dirt, to the extent that he cannot even touch money ("filthy lucre") or door handles, yet is constantly preoccupied with the possibility of being dirtied. A phobia and a compulsive ritual is thus formed. The ideas which have been repressed continue to exist and, because of their connection with the original wishful impulses, strive for expression. At night with the regressive path open, a hallucinatory outlet is provided for them in the form of a dream.

Not all unpleasant experiences will be subject to repression, and not all painful memories are forgotten. But memories which have become associated with those early impulses which were once gratifying, but later repudiated, are subject to the repressive fate. These memories are unique to each person and reflect his own history within his family.

THE CONTINUITY OF NORMALITY AND PSYCHOPATHOLOGY

The psychology of the dreaming process has led to the formulation of:

1. Two kinds of thinking, primary and secondary processes
2. Two systems, a drive and an inhibiting system, and a dynamic relation between them
3. A theory of primitive affects

4. A theory of development
5. A theory of consciousness as a sense organ, separate from perception

These structures and their functioning are not characteristic of only psychopathologically disturbed people; primary process thinking is the kind of thinking that is characteristic of the very young child who is dominated by drives or the older person freed from inhibition. Repression or censorship, too, is part of the normal process of growth. Freud's statement on these issues was quite clear.

> It is not now a question of whether I have formed an approximately correct opinion of the psychological factors with which we are concerned, but whether, which is quite possible in such difficult matters, my picture of them is distorted and incomplete. However many changes may be made in our reading of the psychical censorship and of the rational and abnormal revisions made of the dream content, it remains true that processes of this sort are at work in the formation of dreams and that they show the closest analogy in their essentials to the processes observable in the formation of hysterical symptoms. The dream, however, is no pathological phenomenon; it presupposes no disturbance of psychical equilibrium; it leaves behind it no loss of efficiency. The suggestion may be made that no conclusions as to the dreams of normal people can be drawn from my dreams or those of my patients; but this, I think, is an objection which can be safely disregarded. If then we may argue back from the phenomena to their motive forces, we must recognize that the psychical mechanism employed by neuroses is not created by the impact of a pathological disturbance upon the mind but is present already in the normal structure of the mental apparatus. The two psychical systems, the censorship upon the passage from one of them to the other, the inhibition and overlaying of one activity by the other, the relations of both to the consciousness—or whatever more correct interpretations of the observed facts may take their place—all of these form part of the normal structure of our mental instrument, and dreams show us one of the paths leading to an understanding of its structure [1900, p. 607].

We must again emphasize that the model presented is meant to be a guide to understanding the complexity of man's mind. It is to be accepted as no more than a series of analogies and metaphors. Although Freud developed the model in spatial terms, it could easily be translated into energy terms or, as some are trying to do today, into the language of cybernetics and information theory. Here is Freud's enlightening statement on this matter:

It will be seen on closer consideration that what the psychological discussion in the preceding sections invites us to assume is not the existence of two *systems* near the motor end of the apparatus but the existence of two kinds of processes of *excitation*, or modes of its *discharge*. It is all one to us, for we must always be prepared to drop our conceptual scaffolding if we feel that we are in a position to replace it by something that approximates more closely to the unknown reality. So let us try to correct some conceptions which might be misleading so long as we looked upon the two systems in the most literal and crudest sense as two localities in the mental apparatus—conceptions which have left their traces on the expressions "to repress" and "to force a way through." Thus, we may speak of an unconscious thought seeking to convey itself into the preconscious so as to be able then to force its way through into consciousness. What we have in mind here is not the forming of a second thought situated in a new place, like a transcription which continues to exist alongside the original; and the notion of forcing a way through into consciousness must be kept carefully free from any idea of a change of locality. Again, we may speak of a preconscious thought being repressed or driven out and then taken over by the unconscious. These images, derived from a set of ideas relating to a struggle for a piece of ground, may tempt us to suppose that it is literally true that a mental grouping in one locality has been brought to an end and replaced by a fresh one in another locality. Let us replace these metaphors by something that seems to correspond better to the real state of affairs, and let us say instead that some particular mental grouping has had a cathexis of energy attached to it or withdrawn from it, so that the structure in question has come under the sway of a particular agency or been withdrawn from it. What we are doing here is . . . to replace a topographical way of representing things by a dynamic one. What we regard as mobile is not the psychical structure itself but its innervation [1900, pp. 610–611].

Later changes in the theory—particularly with the publication of "The Ego and The Id" (Freud, 1923) and "Inhibitions, Symptoms and Anxiety" (Freud, 1926)—introduced a view of consciousness as a quality of ideas rather than as a function. Also, the identity of primary process thinking with unconscious psychological processes and secondary process thinking with preconscious psychological processes had to be abandoned as inconsistent with empirical observation, for many instances of primary process thoughts can be conscious. For example, the delusion of one schizophrenic patient that thought waves from Peking were poisoning his food is a primary process formation that shows the illogic, condensation, and displacement typical of such thinking. Yet the patient was quite conscious of it. And secondary process fantasies can be unconscious; for example, the love and hate relationship between a child and his parents and the child's fantasies about that relationship may follow the story-line of a romantic plot. Yet the essential elements of those fantasies are unconscious.

It also became necessary to replace some aspects of the topographic theory with structural concepts; for example, the idea of a struggle between preconscious and unconscious ideas and the censorship of unconscious ideas by a preconscious censor was replaced by a struggle between drives and inhibitory structures (later referred to as *id* and *ego*). Before exploring these revisions, it is best to turn to an exposition of the theory of drives.

Summary

Having elaborated his theory that dreams have motivational significance, Freud attempted to construct a model of the mind that provided for the occurrence of dreams and for the kind of thinking typical of dreams. A first draft of this model in neurological terms had been attempted in 1895, but the complications of such an endeavor were so formidable that Freud abandoned it in favor of a purely psychological effort. The model considered the interrelationships of several psychological processes, including memory, attention, perception, consciousness, censorship, and the motivated activation of each of them. The model also formalized a theoretical dichotomy between a drive system and an inhibiting system, later called *id* and *ego*.

CHAPTER 8

THE DRIVES

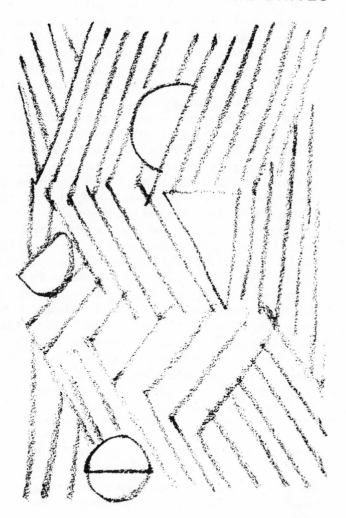

The First Drive Theory

In the previous chapter we discussed the model of the mind that Freud inferred from his examination of dreams and dreaming, phenomena which are part of everyday experiences. We saw that this model requires conflict to activate the mind. The central role in human experience that Freud assigned to conflict emerged from a study of psychopathological phenomena and of neurosis in particular, for it is there that one is struck by inner struggles, suffering, and agonies. Neurotic people will often complain of their exhausting battle against inner compulsions and urges—to flee, to hurt, to ravage, to look, or to avoid. Descriptions of their inner experiences lead one to consider the existence of inner forces or drives which conflict with counterforces, and Freud considered such a construct of drives in his theory of conflict. The psychoanalytic theory of drives, however, grew exceedingly complex as it underwent many revisions. In this chapter we will trace chronologically the various psychoanalytic drive theories—there are four versions—and try to show their relevance for understanding psychopathology.

The basic psychoanalytic model centers on the conflicts implicit in human behavior. In the earliest model, developed in 1894 (Freud, 1894) and 1896 (Freud, 1896), the essential conflict underlying many neurotic symptoms was between a painful memory of a real event and an aspect of one's self-representation. In 1900, as outlined in *The Interpretation of Dreams,* the conflicting forces involved *wishes* and *counter*wishes, neither of which necessarily reflected actual reality events. The former implied the existence of drive-forces or impulses; the latter referred to a system of controlling processes, some of which are described as censorship, defense, repression—that is, processes which served to delay the direct expression of drives by means of thought. In later versions, the conflicting forces were drives and restraining forces.

DRIVES AS ENDOGENOUS STIMULI: PRECURSORS OF THE DRIVE THEORY IN "THE PROJECT"

The nature of the drives, however, was not explored and examined systematically until 1905, when Freud published his "Three Essays on the

Theory of Sexuality." After he had detailed the complicated psychic apparatus in 1900, he next turned his attention to the working out of a theory of drives. The precursors of the theory, to be sure, had been implicit in his writings at least since 1895, when in "The Project" he described motivating forces—internal and external stimuli—arising continually and requiring organismic action to be discharged. These stimuli motivated a discharge process called *emotion* along motor pathways; this discharge, however, could bring relief from the pressure of external stimuli but not from endogenous stimuli. The relief from internal stimuli—like hunger, for example—required an appropriate object from the external world. Freud often used the illustrative example of a hungry infant for whom food was the object that could bring relief from the pressure of the endogenous stimuli experienced as hunger. However, the hungry infant received the food from an adult when he cried or gave some other emotional signal. The food and, by association, the adult brought a temporary end to the hunger stimulation, and the infant experienced satisfaction. Thereafter, whenever the inner stimuli associated with hunger occurred, the infant sought the same need-satisfying object. The motivation which arises connecting the endogenous stimulus and the satisfying object he called a wishful state. Even in *The Interpretation of Dreams*, Freud left vague the specification of the endogenous stimuli; he simply postulated the existence of "wishes" as the ultimate motivators of the mental system.

FROM FANTASIES TO DRIVES

While it is true that Freud had assumed something related to a drive theory in his early works, it was only later, when his clinical experience brought new data and new insights, that an explicit theory was derived inductively from these data and then was integrated with the earlier, more deductive, assumptions.

As mentioned earlier, Freud concluded that although nearly all his patients reported having been seduced, these reports were of fantasies rather than of actual events. When he searched the literature he found many similar reports written by physicians who knew nothing about psychoanalysis or who opposed it, so he considered it improbable that he had suggested the fantasies to his patients. He now required an explanation that would take into account the almost universal presence of these seduction fantasies.

Freud explained their universal appearance by postulating that they were representations of a sexual drive in the form of a thought. Thus, the sexual drive was named as one of the endogenous stimuli which motivated action, thought, and affect. Freud devoted his volume, "Three Essays on the Theory of Sexuality," and several other papers, to working out the theory of the sexual drive and its relationship to another inferred drive, that of self-preservation. A number of important revisions were introduced about 1914 (Freud, 1914b) when Freud became aware that self-preservative and sexual motivations were not conceptually distinct and separate. Finally, in 1920 (Freud, 1920), the range of phenomena relating to aggression and destructiveness was brought into the drive theory. Thus, the final statement of Freud's drive theory embraced the phenomena of sex, aggression, and self-preservation.

Clinical experiences pressed Freud to revise his drive theory several times; indeed, the theory of drives and their classification is still subject to revision. Psychoanalytic theory gives much prominence to drives, particularly sexual and aggressive ones, but it has never proved, and indeed never can, that they are the only, or even the most important, drives. The present psychoanalytic drive theory remains merely one way of interpreting observed phenomena and inner experiences. The inner experiences which are centrally important are motives that have been conceptualized as "sexual and aggressive drives," having sex and aggression as their ultimate aim.[1] New empirical findings in physiology and other biological sciences relevant to the nature and development of drives should be welcomed by psychoanalysis as adding to the knowledge about human behavior, thus leading to changes and further refinement of the theory.

[1] The special theory of specific drive energies—e.g., "libido" and "aggressive energy," often used at present, is not essential to a psychoanalytic drive theory and may be challenged without harm to the theory of drives. As Schafer (1968) has pointed out, the psychoanalytic concept of drive includes both qualitative and quantitative aspects. The quality of a drive refers to the aim of the drive, whether sexual or aggressive; the quantity refers simply to its strength. Schafer suggests that some of the conceptual difficulties of the psychoanalytic drive theory stem from this linking together in one concept both the quantitative and qualitative aspects of drive (1968, chapter 3).

We will use the term *drive* for Freud's German word *Trieb*. *Trieb* has sometimes been translated as *instinct*, yet the terms *Trieb* and *Instinkt* in German have quite different connotations. The latter implies a fixed pattern of response to stimuli—like the web-spinning behavior of a spider. *Trieb*, on the other hand, pertains to a stimulus which creates a demand for some behavioral response. The stimulus is called an *endosomatic* phenomenon—that is, one arising within the body—which can become conscious only through the ideas and affect that become associated with the expression and manifestations of its aims. This is an ambiguous definition, although no vaguer than are many other definitions in other sciences. Freud's ambiguity in the definition of the concept of drive is deliberate, for he wanted to leave room for the concept to be reexamined, modified, and elaborated as further experience accumulated. All that Freud insisted upon was the necessity for assuming an internal motivating source, in contrast to the radical empiricists who viewed the organism as merely the passive recipient and recorder of external experiences. Freud begins his paper "Instincts and Their Vicissitudes" with a methodological argument:

> We have often heard it maintained that sciences should be built upon clear and sharply defined basic concepts. In actual fact no science, not even the most exact, begins with such definitions. The true beginning of scientific activity consists rather in describing phenomena and then in proceeding to group, classify and correlate them. Even at the stage of description it is not possible to avoid applying certain abstract ideas to the material in hand, ideas derived from somewhere or other but certainly not from the new observations alone. Such ideas—which will later become the basic concepts of the science—are still more indispensable as the material is further worked over. They must at first necessarily possess some degree of indefiniteness; there can be no question of any clear delimitation of their content. So long as they remain in this condition, we come to an understanding about their meaning by making repeated references to the material of observation from which they appear to have been derived, but upon which, in fact, they have been imposed. Thus strictly speaking, they are in the nature of conventions—although everything depends on their not being arbitrarily chosen but determined by their having significant relations to the empirical material, relations that we seem to sense before we can clearly rec-

ognize and demonstrate them. It is only after more thorough investigation of the field of observation that we are able to formulate its basic scientific concepts with increased precision, and progressively so to modify them that they become serviceable and consistent over a wide area. Then, indeed, the time may have come to confine them in definitions. The advance of knowledge, however, does not tolerate any rigidity even in definitions. Physics furnishes an excellent illustration of the way in which even "basic concepts" that have been established in the form of definitions are constantly being altered in their content [Freud, 1914, p. 117].

Like external stimuli, drive stimuli arise and create a demand for response or put in motion a set of behaviors that ultimately can ensure the cessation of such stimuli. Freud's concept of drive implies only an internal excitation that requires "discharge." It does not imply fixed unlearned responses or fixed relationships to outside objects. The earliest response of the mental apparatus to the drive stimulus is regulated by an organismic principle—called the *pleasure principle*—which requires immediate discharge of the drive. As we discussed in Chapter 7, immediate discharge is unadaptive, and therefore a new regulating principle—the *reality principle*—is required. This second or reality principle also ensures reduction of tension in the long run, although it does so via delays and detours in reality. There are, of course, exceptions to the rule that all action motivated by drives is designed to reduce tension. Some motivated action, such as foreplay in the sexual act, raises tension or keeps excitement at a particular level. There is thus a distinction between engaging in activities which directly reduce drive tension (by way of the pleasure principle) and engaging in other behavior, which is also inspired by drives but which does not have as its aim the immediate reduction of the drive tension.

THE BROADENED VIEW OF SEXUALITY

Freud elaborated his theory of the sexual drives after he became convinced that the ubiquitous conflict in neurosis was between sexual urges and forces which control or reject them. The regular appearance of sexual fantasies in his patients led to the explanation that there was a universal, inexorable sexual urge which, although unlearned, was nevertheless shaped by experiences.

But what is to be considered sexual? It is clearly not just "reproduction." Even if one takes as a criterion those activities involved in the so-called sex act, one finds among such acts many behaviors not involved in reproduction which we nonetheless consider unmistakably sexual. Much of what is termed foreplay involves not just the primary reproductive organs, but other parts of the body as well: the skin, the mouth, the anus, the breasts. Furthermore, the "perversions" are not connected with reproduction, but we call them sexual nonetheless. Perverse activities include those in which the sexual object has been altered, the focus of interest being in other parts of the body, such as the mouth or anus rather than on the genital organs. In still other perversions, ultimate sexual enjoyment is found even in pieces of clothing. There are perversions in which the goal is that of looking at or displaying parts of the body and achieving orgasm by engaging in sadistic and masochistic behavior.

Reports of these perverse practices exist from the earliest recorded history of all cultures and civilizations. They support the view that other parts of the body can acquire the significance of genital organs and that a sexual connotation can exist simultaneously with the intended anatomical function of certain nongenital bodily parts. The reader can find considerably more information on the psychoanalytic views of sexual perversions in Freud's "Three Essays on the Theory of Sexuality," and in some recent works on sexual aberrations.

THE ONTOGENETIC DEVELOPMENT OF SEXUALITY

This widened view of sexuality—that genital sexual activity does not encompass all of sexuality—is further extended by observations of children and by retrospective reports of patients about their childhood. Such data confirm the view that there is an early independence of sexuality and reproduction, since sexual activity can be observed long before biological maturity. Today, unlike the days when Freud first proposed his views, it is no longer necessary to argue the point that sexual behavior does not make its first appearance during puberty. Observations of unmistakable masturbatory activity in children are no longer disputed. But activities involving the phallus in boys and the clitoris in little girls do not exhaust the range of children's sexual behavior. Pleasure in nonnutritive sucking and anal activities are also acknowledged as related to sexuality in infants and young children as they are in adult perversions. There seems to be a developmental sequence in the appearance of parts of the body that yield pleasure to the child: first the mouth is the center of attention, then the anus, then the genitals.

Infantile sexual activities do not involve other people but only parts of the infant's own body and are thus termed *autoerotic*. Some of the infantile activities can be seen as counterparts of the adult perversions. Indeed, the sexual life and interests of children can be called "perverse" because children do not have the capacity for mature genital behavior that leads to reproduction. When finally the reproductive capacity is mature, the infantile perverse sexual trends which are superseded do not disappear but persist and are organized in the service of the aim of normal genital union, as for example, in foreplay.

Freud formulated the theory of sexuality from three sources of data:

1. Considerations of sexual perversions
2. The memories of adult patients (during the course of their psychoanalysis) of their childhood sexual activities
3. Direct observations of children

The theory insists that a sexual drive is one of the important impulses in human life, that it is manifestly present from early infancy, and that its source is somatic. In the course of development, its center changes from the mouth to the anus to the genitals. The first manifestations of sexuality occur in association with nutritional activities—the taking in and, later, the chewing of food. For example, sucking is at first linked with feeding but is engaged in independently, as an end in itself. This phase is called the *oral phase* of psychosexual development. Still later sexual pleasure is linked to the functions of excretion—which yield pleasure through the stimulation of the anal and urethral mucuous membranes. This phase is called the *anal phase* of psychosexual development.[2] Soon the dominant concern shifts from pleasure in sensations from oral and anal sources to pleasure in sensations from the genital organs; autoerotic activity and gratification take the form of genital mas-

[2] Social demands for inhibition and control first center around these excretory functions. Therefore, issues of power, control, responsibility, compliance, and defiance first arise in association with the social requirements made during the anal phase. The control of other striated muscle systems—those used in locomotion, for example—also begin to develop at this time, and these, too, become associated with the increasing social demands for control, inhibition, and delay.

turbation. This phase is called the *phallic phase* of psychosexual development. Fantasies concerning childbirth and sexual activities, particularly those imagined to be taking place between the parents, become prominent. Personal anxieties—in some boys about the integrity of their penis and in some girls about their disappointment in not having a penis—are discernible at this time.

The sexual drive, thus, does not first appear as mature genitality but develops in a series of phases, each of which has its period of maximum ascendancy. A controversial aspect of this theory concerns the postulation of an energic quantity—*libido*—to account for the force of the sexual drive. The term "libido" was first used in its original Latin connotation to describe genital desire and excitement and thus referred to a psychological experience. As he worked out his sexual drive theory, Freud applied the term to the hypothetical energy of the sexual drive. Thus the *"quantitative* factor" referred to in "The Project" and the "endogenous stimulation" referred to in chapter VII of *The Interpretation of Dreams* were now identified and given a label: libido. The term was introduced to explain the observation that sexual objects can become interchangeable, and one sexual aim can be substituted for another. Freud believed that he needed a quantitative entity that could explain not only these substitutions of sexual aims and objects but also the increase and decrease of sexual interest. However, he identified this quantity as having a specific quality, which was sexual. The coupling of these two requirements—the quantitative dimension and the qualitative content of interests—created much conceptual difficulty, particularly when more than one drive was postulated.

The theory of sexuality assumed that libido arises in various parts of the body and has the aim of being discharged via the appropriate objects. Libido may, however, be prevented from being discharged along regular routes by inhibitory processes; under the regulation of the pleasure principle, it will, therefore, seek other ways for discharge. If previously established objects should not be available or should be denied by external or internal prohibitions, a substitute object will be sought. Thus the meaning of neurotic symptoms, which so often in patients' associations betray a sexual significance, was now to be found in the diversion of libido from its aim or object. A case example may serve to illustrate the phenomenon.

A thirty-year-old woman experienced dreadful anxiety attacks whenever she had to sign her name with a pen in the presence of other people. The patient's free associations during her analytic treatment led to her recalling that when she was five years old she would watch her father signing checks. She envied both his ability to write and his general competence, and she wished that she could become as efficient as her father. Other associations linked the connotation of a pen with that of a penis, not only because of the pen's shape, but also because fluid came out of its point. The patient could also recall her unbridled envy of boys and later of men, and for many years she experienced very strong urges to hold and handle a penis. The connections between the patient's symptom, the symbolic significance of the pen, her recollection of her father, her own sexual urges, and the nature of the competitive relationship with men were discovered by her only during her analytic therapy.

This brief excerpt from a case record illustrates not only the sexual significance of the symptom but the sexual quality of the relationship that existed between father and daughter. It cannot be denied that retrospective distortion may have been at work in this instance. Yet, in all psychoanalytic case studies of neurotic patients, the sexual nature of the relationship between mother and son and father and daughter can be discovered. Freud called this relationship the *Oedipus complex* because it seemed to recapitulate the Sophoclean drama in which Oedipus is horrified to discover that he has unknowingly murdered his father and married his mother. Naturally the drama is not literally repeated in each life; but the mutual attraction between mother and son and between father and daughter, and the corresponding rivalry between father and son and mother and daughter has been reconstructed from psychoanalyses and from observations of children. Although these tendencies are controlled by repression or other defensive techniques, significant residues remain. The pattern of relationship toward the opposite sex is molded to a considerable extent by experiences during the oedipal struggles, whereas patterns of behavior toward members of the same sex are based on a residue of unconscious guilt for the hostile wishes directed toward the parent of the same sex. Many inhibitions of sexual functioning, avoidance of or flights into marriage, and choice of marriage partner can be traced to the unique outcome of each patient's oedipal conflicts.

EGO DRIVES

In his first drive theory Freud called the forces opposing the sexual drive *ego drives* or *self-preservative drives*. He sometimes also referred to these as *ego interests*. This dichotomy of sexual versus ego drives, however, was deliberately left as a provisional classification to be modified as required by empirical data. The ego drives were considered to include attitudes, goals, sentiments, as well as tendencies toward mastery and competence. But these nonsexual motivations were not yet to be the focus of psychoanalytic study and they were, therefore, neglected until 1923 when Freud began to examine the controlling structures of the mind. Thus from 1905 until the publication of "The Ego and the Id" (Freud, 1923), the ego drives were simply postulated as those forces opposed to the sexual drive. Some of the serious quarrels within the psychoanalytic movement, such as Freud's disputes with Adler and Jung, were over the early neglect of these nonsexual factors. Adler, for example, insisted that the crucial factor in neurosis was the frustration of the ego drives for mastery, rather than that of the sexual drives. Jung insisted upon a single drive theory which would reduce sexual and nonsexual motivations to a single and undifferentiated energy. Both addressed themselves to aspects of the theory that required revision: for Adler, the modulating structures, and for Jung, the relationship between sexual urges and lofty aspirations, as well as the conceptual ambiguity of a quantitative element—energy—that had specific content or quality.

THE ONTOGENETIC DEVELOPMENT OF THE EGO DRIVES

Freud argued that just as the sexual drive developed through a series of stages, the ego drives also unfolded epigenetically. But he did not work out these stages of development except for the theory of *fixation and regression* (see page 120) which encompassed both sexual and ego drives. While he considered the energy of both drives to be capable of fixation and regression, the theory was worked out principally for the libido theory. The stages of ego development and their coordination with sexual development were to be detailed by Erik Erikson many years later (Erikson, 1963). Freud's early neglect of the ego factors probably reflected more the sources from which data of the psychoanalytic studies came than from any denial on his part of the importance of those modulating and controlling factors. In the early years of psychoanalysis he was concerned with the study of the so-called defense neuroses which called attention to the sexual conflicts of the sufferers and made it necessary to postulate the existence of a sexual drive. Later, his study of other pathological conditions, particularly psychoses, called attention to the crucial role of factors other than drives, particularly ego factors (e.g., Freud, 1911a, 1924). Freud had left the door open to revisions of theory required by the new data from those studies. In one of his lectures on psychoanalysis in 1916–1917, he told his audience:

> Nor can I think it would be a disaster to the trend of our researches if what lies before us is the discovery that in severe psychoses the ego instincts have gone astray as a primary fact. The future will give the answer—to you at any rate [1916–1917, p. 430].

DRIVES AND NEUROSIS: FIXATION AND REGRESSION

While the theory of an epigenetic development of sexual drive organization implies a regular and progressive unfolding of successive stages, it does not require that a precise time schedule of drive development be followed. In some instances, stages may not be reached on time; in other instances, stages may be only incompletely attained. For example, some of the energy (libido) of the sexual drive may remain fixed at earlier stages, on zones associated with early aims, or on drive-related objects which are no longer age appropriate. The term given to this phenomenon is *fixation*. It refers to those situations in which the sexual drive has remained focused on earlier developmental levels, the so-called pregenital stages, rather than progressing toward mature genitality. The phenomenon of fixation as a major factor in the etiology of neurosis, particularly of hysteria and obsessive-compulsive neurosis, will be discussed in Chapter 9.

Freud's theory maintains that when part of the libido remains fixated at earlier stages, there is an increased likelihood that at a later period some of the libido which has progressed farther along in epigenetic development will return to the fixation point. Thus, under certain conditions, there will be a *regression* of the sexual drive from advanced positions to earlier aims and objects. The idea of a tendency toward sexual regression to earlier and simpler levels is analogous to Hughlings Jackson's (1931) model in which "lower," older, and more primitive neural systems are conceived of as continuing to exist under the domination of "higher," more recently evolved and complex systems; these lower systems can be restored to dominance with injury to the higher system. Thus, in hysteria the libido is presumed to regress to the objects and aims of the oedipal phase of development. This retreat from the aims and objects of genital maturity implies a return to incestuous object choices and triggers the expression of those earlier urges and, with it, conflicts about their expression. In obsessional and compulsive disorders, the retreat is to the anal phase of development with intense interest paid to issues of control, power, magical manipulation, and ambivalence. Regression of libido is as important as fixation in the etiology of these two neuroses.

For regression to occur, according to Freud, the sexual drive must be frustrated in real life. How much frustration is required to trigger a regression will depend upon prior fixation. If the fixation is minor, a greater amount of frustration is required; conversely, if the fixation is major, a trivial amount of frustration may trigger a regression. Once a regression has occurred, the person resorts to earlier modes of drive satisfaction appropriate to the phase to which the regression has occurred.

Here is one such example.

A thirty-two-year-old teacher began to show overt signs of transvestite behavior. Intermittently, he would feel an inner compulsion to dress in women's clothes, go out on the street, and attempt to attract the attention of both men and women. He was able to convince his wife to help him in these adventures, and she began to purchase clothes and wigs for him. These nocturnal adventures many times culminated in his having sexual relations with his wife, provided he wore a woman's nightgown.

The patient was born to a woman in her mid-forties who clearly resented her pregnancy, the more so because he was not a girl. She gave him a name usually given to girls, approved only of soft, feminine behavior, reprimanded him for boyish rowdiness and intrusiveness. She dominated and intimidated her husband who sought respite from his shrewish wife in solitary fishing expeditions and who thus spent little time with his son. The patient's early history clearly shows an unusual emphasis on feminine behavior; indeed, it appeared that the mother granted or withheld affection according to how much the patient succeeded in acting like a girl. Whatever feminine characteristics were present in the boy's temperament were cultivated to the point that they became dominant in his early childhood. Although when the boy went to school these feminine qualities were subdued, the early excesses and experiences created a fixation on transvestite tendencies.

The patient's academic career was not noteworthy; he finally was graduated from college, and he obtained a teaching license. He did well as a teacher and was rewarded with an appointment as a principal of an elementary school. His first assignment as principal was to a school where all the teachers were women. After a few months there, he grew uncomfortable with these women whom he regarded as aggressive and shrewish. He soon began to show signs of anxiety, and his work efficiency began to diminish. After about a year in his position as principal, he began to experience the urges to dress as a woman. This situation was clearly reminiscent of his early relationship with his own mother, and it revived in him the complex feelings of love and hate he felt toward his mother. His earlier feminine behavior—now labeled a perverse symptom—reestablished itself as a regressive response to his current, frustrating life situation.

If the ego drives find these modes acceptable, perverse sexual behavior such as the above or other infantile characteristics will occur. If, however, the ego interests which have attained a higher developmental level judge these regressed trends to be incompatible with the interests of reality and the self, a conflict between the sexual and ego drives will ensue. The regressive wishes or their ideational derivatives are then repressed by virtue of their connection with previous unconscious and repressed drive derivatives. Just as dream thoughts are transformed by the dream work, so are unacceptable regressive wishes subjected to the distortions of condensation, displacement, and other modes of the primary process. Under the regulation of the pleasure principle, however, the regressed drive derivatives continue to see expression and may eventually emerge in the form of a compromise between the ego interests and the regressed sexual drive. This compromise, which distorts both sides of the conflict, emerges as the neurotic symptom.

Here is another clinical example.

When the patient was 21 and a senior in a large university, his father suddenly died. Four months later, while presiding at a large meeting of students, the patient suffered an anxiety attack. He felt faint, and had a strong urge to run from the room, but was unable to do so. The experience left him shaken but within a few days he forgot about it. He went on to do excellent postgraduate work in accounting and was then drafted into the Army. He rose to the rank of captain and served creditably in an administrative capacity.

Shortly after his discharge from the Army, and about nine years after his first anxiety attack, the patient, as he described the situation, "found himself engaged" to a vivacious, pretty girl. The girl, he said, took all the initiative in deciding upon the engagement and in arranging the details of the marriage; he himself had simply acquiesced. A few days after his engagement the patient experienced his second severe attack of anxiety, but this time it was followed by a rapidly expanding phobic syndrome. What at first was only episodic spells of fear became incapacitating within two weeks. He was unable to go anywhere without his fiancée, and soon even her presence ceased to reassure him.

During the psychoanalytic treatment the patient discovered that he had as a child sensed his father's weakness and feared to become a self-sufficient person who might challenge his father's authority, all the while, wishing to do just that, but with manifest guilt. He realized that the first anxiety attack had taken place immediately after an envied mentor had told him that he would be leaving the university and that the patient should carry on for him; he connected this with the death of his father which left him wishing to replace his father but guilty over the wish. The second and disabling attack occurred at the point in his life when he seemed about to become a husband, a father, and, symbolically, an adult. Its occurrence in the face of an impending marriage signaled his general retreat from mature acceptance of heterosexuality. Marriage, as the embodiment of many of those urges to replace his father that tempted and alarmed him, had to be indefinitely postponed. But the aggression in this instance conflicted with the wishes of the adult side of the patient [Holzman, 1964].

In this process of neurotic symptom formation, it is only certain specific frustrations which trigger the neurotic process. The specific frustrations differ from one person to another and are related to the individual's unconscious conflicts rooted in his critical childhood years. Furthermore, neither frustration in real life nor the ensuing regression necessarily produce a clinical neurosis. An even more important factor may be the internal conflict made more intense by the regression: the conflict between the sexual drives and the self-preservative interests.

PRIMARY AND SECONDARY GAINS OF NEUROSIS

Although the neurotic symptom brings suffering and pain to the patient, it also provides him with the *primary gain* of drive gratification. A neurotic symptom in the psychoanalytic view always represents an attempt to gratify an infantile unconscious aim. Like a dream, the symptom thus represents a wish fulfillment. In many instances it is also possible to discover a *secondary* gain from the illness when, in addition to the primary aim, the patient earns an added advantage from the neurotic disability. For example, a man's neurotic sexual impotence may elicit from his sexually uninterested wife a gratifying display of pity, compassion, and tender nurturing, which the patient, when potent, had been unable to elicit from her.[3]

THE "COMPLEMENTARY SERIES"

Psychoanalytic theory explicitly denies that any single factor, constitutional or experiential, is the cause of neurosis. It maintains that neurosis is determined by at least three sets of relationships between factors. Freud referred to each set as a "complementary series" by which he meant that the elements or factors in each set were complementary to one another. Qualitatively, then, the more of one factor that was present, the less of another was required to produce a given effect. The word "series" referred to all the possible different combinations of factors in a given set.

First, Freud described a complementary series between constitutional endowment and infantile experience in causing fixations: Constitutional dispositions toward a strong oral or anal drive required less intense experiential factors to produce anal or oral fixations, while with weaker drives, more intense experiences were needed.

Second, he described the relationship between the amount of pre-existing fixation and the amount of frustrating experiences required to

[3] These strong secondary gains may make the patient's treatment difficult. If the main force perpetuating the neurosis is its original motivation, therapeutic attention paid only to the secondary gains will often be unsuccessful. On the other hand, if the primary motivation of the illness is no longer active and the neurotic pattern is maintained by the secondary gains, attention to those secondary factors—for example, characteristic styles of relationships with people—may give crucial therapeutic leverage. Many theories of neurosis have been formulated that emphasize the secondary gains of neurosis, particularly the ways in which people exploit each other (e.g., Berne, 1964). These theories are clearly relevant only to cases of the second type. Psychoanalysis regards these exploitative transactions as truly secondary complications of neurosis rather than its primary cause.

produce regressions to fixated positions. In some cases, the childhood experiences are the overwhelmingly important factors and adult experiences seem minimal in producing regressions. It is as if such people would have fallen ill whatever the circumstances. In other cases, the reverse is true; for the frustrations in adulthood seem to be the more important factor, and the fixations during the person's maturational history seem to be almost without significance.

Third, there is the relationship between the importance in a person's life of fantasies about infantile and childhood sexuality and actual childhood sexual experiences. It is the fantasies, rather than recollections about actual events, that represent in a person's mind the pregenital sexual phases; it is these fantasies which can be reactivated after frustrating reality experiences. The reactivation of these fantasies by the "retreating libido" intensifies their significance, and they can become a source of internal discomfort. For example, the woman who could not sign her name in public experienced a reactivation of her very intense childhood fantasies about her father—jealousy of his power, envy of his skill, romantic love, childish affections, and fantasy of replacing him by becoming like him. Thus, if childhood sexual fantasies have been strong, little needs to have actually taken place for these fantasies to be revived in times of stress.

The concept of complementary series implicates several of the points of view required by a psychoanalytic explanation of behavior:

1. The dynamic view—that of motivation and of conflict between motives
2. The genetic view—that of the history of the individual, particularly of those events whose outcome is the establishment of fixations
3. The topographic view—that of the unconscious and preconscious status of drive derivatives
4. The economic view—that of the relative intensities of forces, whether genetic and experiential, sexual and nonsexual, fantasied and real

The Second Version of the Drive Theory

By 1914 Freud found it difficult to maintain the antithesis between sexual and ego drives, particularly in the face of clinical evidence from three sources, all of which suggested that self-interest was not as devoid of sexual aims as he had first thought: (1) The study of homosexuals impressed him with the intensity of their self-love; thus one's self-regard or self-esteem seemed to have a sexual component; (2) experience with schizophrenic patients, particularly those with paranoid symptoms, brought evidence of their megalomanic fantasies, suggesting a kind of "sexualization" or "libidinization" of their thoughts; (3) observations of children suggested that they characteristically overvalue the effects of their wishes and thoughts. These phenomena suggested that preoccupation with self and overestimation of one's own importance—a phase of self-love—may be a normal feature of development and that it may recur in pathological states in adult life, as in organic illness and hypochondriasis in which the patient is self-centered, no longer interested in other people or things. Freud called this self-love *narcissism*, after Narcissus who, in the Greek myth, fell in love with his own image reflected in a pool. It seemed to Freud that if one might direct libidinal strivings toward oneself in the form of self-love, it was no longer tenable to postulate a strict separation of the libidinal (sexual) drives and ego drives or self-preservative drives. He therefore speculated that there was a relatively fixed quantity of libido available at any given time and that, thus, the more libido that one invested in others, the more depleted was the supply available for oneself, and vice versa. "Narcissistic libido" (invested in oneself) and "object libido" (invested in others) were thus inversely related.[4] The distinction between the ego and sexual drives was further blurred by Freud's new postulate that at least in the early stages of development, the same energy powered the sexual and ego drives. This new assumption weakened Freud's first drive theory which insisted on qualitatively different energies for sexual and ego drives. There seemed now to be only one group of drives, all fueled by libido.

But Freud continued to adhere to the weakened dichotomy between sexual and ego drives, in part because he wanted to keep the biological distinction between preservation of species and the preservation of the individual, and in part because he still needed, conceptually, to postulate a structure which was attuned to reality, which stood in opposition to the sexual drive, and which had its own source of energy.

[4] For a careful and clinically useful examination of narcissism in the context of contemporary psychoanalytic thinking, see Kohut (1966, 1968).

The Third Version of the Drive Theory

The drive theory as it existed in 1914 (Freud, 1914) gave a prominent place to the erotic impulses and their vicissitudes, but little place to aggression. Aggressive behavior was taken account of only in sadism and masochism as perverse manifestations of the sexual drive and in defenses or aggressive self-preservation as manifestations of the ego drives. Four additional observations of aggressive behavior needed to be accounted for by the drive theory, and in 1917 Freud encompassed them in his third version of the theory of drives. Freud's solution in this third version was to subsume aggressive motivations under the self-preservation drives.

1. The first observation was that oral, anal, and phallic behavior had aggressive and destructive components. In children, the aggressiveness of chewing and biting, the stubbornness of fecal retention or the defiance of fecal expulsion, and competitiveness of exhibitionism and rivalry were noted.
2. The second observation embraced sadistic and masochistic behavior. Freud observed much wanton cruelty that seemed not to be accompanied by sexual orgastic reactions and much self-directed aggression, such as hair-pulling and head-banging; these, too, seemed to be independent of erotic motivations.
3. The third observation was of behavior involving control, mastery, dominance, and power, all of which implicated aggression without considerations of libido or sexual motives.
4. The fourth observation, already accounted for in his 1914 drive theory, was of aggressive behavior in the service of self-protection.

These four observations all showed aggressive behavior to be as varied as sexual behavior. At times, aggressive and sexual impulses seemed to be fused, presenting either a positive picture, as in the case of genital potency, or a negative one, as in sadistic perversion. At other times, the aggressive impulses seemed to be quite independent of sexual impulses. Freud's third version of his drive theory incorporated aggressive impulses but provisionally assigned them to the self-preservation drives, to maintain the dual drive theory. This proved to be an inadequate solution.

The Fourth Version of the Drive Theory

By 1923 Freud had been confronted with other observations that made it necessary to revise the classification of drives. He now considered drives to be of two kinds, sexual and aggressive; he subsumed the self-preservative interests, previously considered drives, under a new organization which he called the *ego*. The essential opposition between drives (sex and aggression), on the one hand, and control structures (ego), on the other, was maintained in this revision, but he now conceptualized the drive functions as having an organized structure called the *id*. The observations that led to these changes in theory were the following:

In clinical conditions such as depressions, patients reproached themselves with an extraordinary harshness that led to relentless suffering and even suicide.

Some people, not clinically depressed, repeatedly managed to get into situations that brought suffering or punishment to themselves and others.

During the aftermath of traumatic occurrences such as war experiences, the victim relived in fantasy and in dreams the fright and pain of the trauma.

These observations suggested to Freud that aggressive behavior, independent of sexual impulses, existed outside the realm of self-preservative functions and could even threaten the life of the individual. Since he now regarded the sexual and aggressive drives as separate from the self-preservative functions, he was obliged to conceptualize a separate structure that contained them. The ultimate motivation of all activity was presumed to issue from the energy of the two recognized drives of this structure, the id.

Since the pleasure principle demands avoidance of all painful environmental stimuli and discharge of any endogenous increase in unpleasure, Freud's observation of purposeful self-directed aggression clearly required for its explanation a principle of regulation that superseded or went beyond the pleasure principle. Freud made a further speculative leap in assuming that the libidinal drives required a different regulatory principle from the aggressive drives. The sexual drive was seen to be governed by the pleasure principle as modified by the reality principle; the aggressive drive was governed by a tendency to conservation and even to *catabolism*, a tendency to return the organism to previous states of adaptation. Indeed, he considered that if the earliest state of the organism was an inanimate one, the regulatory principle of the aggressive drive called for a return to that state of death. Thus the formulation of two principles of *anabolism* and *catabolism*, of synthesis and disintegration, was finally conceptualized as the *life instinct* and the *death instinct*. These considerations, however, were far from the clinical data and represented Freud's philosophic sweep which he permitted expression only after his sixty-fourth year.

Much of the conceptual difficulty of the several drive theories stems from Freud's attempt to identify a separate qualitative energy with each of the drives: libido and aggression. Schafer (1968) has attempted to clarify the theory by returning to the position that psychic energy is not differentiated but is unitary, having only quantity, and that qualitative differences, such as a sexual or aggressive "quality," can be more properly understood to be related to aims and motives and not to be related to the energy proper. He argues that psychoanalytic theory would gain, rather than lose, by giving up the concept of qualitatively different energies.

Summary

Freud's theory of drive motivations underwent at least four revisions. Even in his earliest theoretical efforts, he postulated some internal activating agent which he called *endogenous* stimulation—in addition to external stimuli—that motivated behavior. The first drive theory identified the internal "endogenous stimuli" as components of a sexual drive which often conflicted with a self-preservative drive. The second drive theory represented an attempt to recognize that self-preservation and sexual motivation often coincided, particularly in such phenomena as self-love and self-esteem. A third revision of Freud's theory of drives was based on the recognition that aggressive motives played a large role in neurotic behavior; this revision subsumed aggressive drives under the self-preservative ones. The fourth version provided for a conceptual separation of sexual from aggressive drives. The structural organization of the drives was called the "id." The drives were modulated by a controlling structure called the "ego." In a speculative sweep, Freud further generalized the sexual and aggressive drives into two basic regulatory tendencies of the organism: to build up and synthesize (anabolism) versus to conserve or to tear down (catabolism), or life and death instincts. Freud's various theories of internal motivation always contained a key variable of a quantitative force; the model of its functioning was that of drive reduction through discharge of its quantity. The models, embedded as they were in the nineteenth-century physicalist tradition, were and are still constantly strained by clinical observations. The clinical observations on which the drive theories were based—the plasticity of sexual and aggressive behavior—remain the hallmarks of a psychoanalytic psychology.

CHAPTER 9

THE EGO

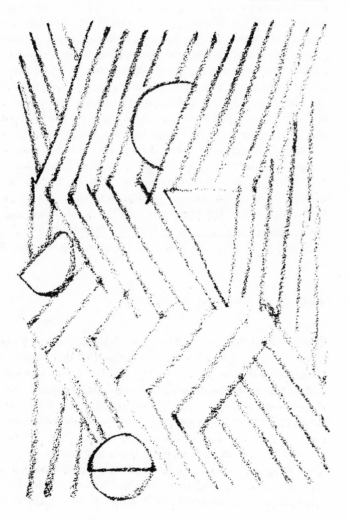

When we talk about the "ego" in psychoanalysis we are referring to a set of psychological functions which include memory, perception, anticipation, and concept formation. These functions are "used" in adapting to external conditions and in controlling and steering drive-related motives. They can thus be used for adaptive or defensive purposes. Aspects of these modulatory processes had been, since the late nineteenth century, the concern of psychologists such as William James in the United States, Wundt and Ebbinghaus in Germany, and Brentano and Ach in Austria. These men studied basic psychological processes such as perception, learning, action, memory, and volition, processes through which drives and motives are expressed and by which they are controlled and steered. The efforts of these men, however, were rather encapsulated, and the theories were fenced off from each other and were unrelated to a general theory of human behavior. We have pointed out that in his early writings, Freud, too, was interested in these various modulatory functions, and in "The Project," in *The Interpretation of Dreams,* and in a few scattered papers such as "Formulations on the Two Principles of Mental Functioning" (1911b), he laid the groundwork for a general psychology of processes involved in adaptive and defensive behavior. Until 1920, however, the development and progressive modification of the drive theory preempted Freud's time and attention, thus preventing him from building a more general psychological theory.

Defects of the First Ego Model

The model worked out in *The Interpretation of Dreams* contained a number of defects. One was the assumption that there was a one-to-one correlation between the system *Ucs* and the drives and between the system *Pcs* and the modulating and controlling processes. Another was the assumption that primary process thinking was typical of the contents only of the Unconscious and secondary process thinking was typical only of Preconscious contents. Freud soon realized that the modulating processes which he had placed in the Preconscious system were in many instances themselves unavailable to consciousness. He also noted that there were fantasies, such as oedipal fantasies, which had the logical organization characteristic of secondary process thinking, but which were unconscious (see Chapter 8); and there were ideas organized according to the primary process which were preconscious.

The effort to remedy these defects actually began in 1920 when Freud reformulated the drive theory in terms of two drives, sexual and aggressive. However, the effort was not successful until Freud restudied the functions of drive modulation and conceived a new theory. This new theory of drive modulation appeared in "The Ego and the Id" and "Inhibitions, Symptoms and Anxiety." The ideas contained in these two works are referred to as the *structural theory* and sometimes as the theory of *ego psychology*. The structures referred to were the *ego*, the *id*, and the *superego*. Thus, although the roots of ego psychological concepts existed as early as 1895, it was not until the enunciation of the structural theory that these concepts became useful and powerful tools. The structural theory provided a new perspective, and it encompassed phenomena, such as the organization of thought, previously at the fringe of psychoanalytic thinking. It also gave impetus to the observation of new data, such as the social behavior of man, which in turn brought modifications and enrichments of the theory. It suggested new formulations of clinical concepts and phenomena, principally of anxiety and the superego, and a widened scope of psychoanalysis to include issues in individual psychological development, such as the individual's relations to his society that could not be undertaken so long as attention was focused almost exclusively on the drives. Some of these extensions will be discussed in Chapter 10.

The Structural Theory

In the structural theory Freud proposed two systems called the *id* and the *ego*. The id was the name given to the reservoir of wishful impulses or the drives—the ultimate motivational source of behavior. The ego comprised an organization of functions involved in control over the drives, as well as other functions not so directly involved. The drives of the id are unconscious not only in a descriptive sense but also in a dynamic sense in that their access to consciousness is actively opposed. The ego, too, has large areas which cannot easily become conscious, although other large areas can. Whereas consciousness in the topographic model was regarded as a function, in this new model it became a quality describing the appearance and disappearance of ideas. Thus, ideas can be of three qualities: unconscious, preconscious, and conscious. The unconscious is restricted to *dynamically* repressed contents, those ideas whose access to consciousness is actively opposed, and the preconscious to contents that are *descriptively* unconscious, that is to ideas that can, without much effort, become conscious.

In the structural model, the repressing forces are assigned to the ego and are considered to be *dynamically* unconscious. This means that they can become conscious only when considerable efforts have been made at removing the defensive opposition to them, in contrast to *descriptively* unconscious ideas which can be made conscious at will.

EFFECTS ON PSYCHOANALYTIC TECHNIQUE

The formulation of the structural theory had significant effects on the technique of psychoanalytic treatment. In the 1890s, psychotherapeutic efforts focused on recovering the memory of the alleged reality trauma. With the discovery that the patient's reports might be fantasies, psychoanalytic efforts were directed toward discovering, by the method of free association, those fantasies and wishful ideas which the patient could not permit himself to express directly and which, through compromise, could be expressed only through neurotic symptoms. The resistances of the patient against discovering these disturbing components of himself then presented a most formidable therapeutic problem. Since the patient seemingly was unaware not only of the wishful impulses and fantasies but also of the fact that he was vigorously resisting recognizing them, Freud, in 1914 (Freud, 1914a), had suggested that the psychoanalyst should first analyze the presence and nature of the repressing or defending forces. Only when this was done could one proceed to analyze the repressed wishes and ideas. With the final formulation of the structural theory (Freud, 1926), the psychoanalysis of patients became increasingly concerned with the defensive strategies of patients (identified as part of the ego) and with the integration of these defensive strategies into aspects of their character structure.

THE EGO AND CONFLICT RESOLUTION: THE SYNTHETIC FUNCTION

The "ego," thus, is the name Freud gave to a particular organized arrangement of mental functions. Freud's term was the common German word, *das Ich,* the "I." He had used the term in a similar way in his 1895 "Project." By referring to a group of mental functions by such a personal term as "I," he underscored his conviction that people can be identified by their unique forms of thought organization. Freud included in the list of functions subsumed under the term "ego:" perception, consciousness, drive-modulating functions, memory, judgment, and concentration. He considered that the stylistic patterning of these functions was idiosyncratic for each person. The fact that the arrangement of these functions was organized and "coherent," in Freud's terms, implied a tendency toward the elimination of conflict. For purposes of exposition, we can describe the differences between the organization within the realm of id and ego anthropomorphically: the id tends to tolerate contradictory impulses, such as love and hate, toward the same person, while the ego tends to level and reconcile such discrepancies. This is a more picturesque but less scientific way of stating that the organized and organizing nature of ego functions is assumed to have a conflict-resolving tendency. This tendency is referred to as the *synthetic function* of the ego.

THE DEVELOPMENT OF THE EGO

The introduction of the concept of the ego inevitably raised the issue of the ego's origin and development. Freud assumed that it developed from the impact on the organism of two sets of forces. The first set is composed of the *drives,* particularly as their object representations (the internal picture of those people and things that satisfy the drives) become modified by experience. The second set is made up of *reality,* as the organism perceives it. Thus, Freud regarded the ego as developing from the pressure of drives and from the effects of contact with the external world as filtered through the perceptual functions. Perception, an inborn capacity, thus ensures the control and eventual satisfaction of drives, another inborn capacity. Freud made no sharp differentiation between the id and the ego in the early development of the person. Nor did he conceive of any basic conflict between id and ego functions, for while the ego controls and modulates drives by virtue of reality's requirements, it does so to gratify drives by eventually finding appropriate objects in reality.

A central aspect of the ego as a modulating structure is its defensive function. This is represented by a congeries of behavior that can be recruited for defensive purposes. As already mentioned, these defenses are not usually conscious and require special work to become so. Thus, included in the dynamically unconscious are not only ideas that have been repressed and aspects of impulses that have never been conscious, but also behaviors and attitudes that maintain repression. In actual clinical practice, one discovers a hierarchy of defenses in which each defense defends against awareness of other defenses. A clinical example may illustrate this point.

The patient we discussed in Chapter 8 (page 122) was a highly intelligent man who was intellectually inhibited and avoided intellectual pursuits because they represented an area of competition with his father, a successful writer. Although he wished to be more successful than his father, he feared the fulfillment of this wish. Suspecting that his father had serious but subtle weaknesses, the patient had to curb his sharp intellect which might have led him to surpass his father. But this defended-against wish to outdo his father was, in turn, a defense against a still earlier childhood fear of his father's strength. His later fear that his father might be weak and needed to be protected thus was a defense against an earlier fear that his father might be insuperably strong.

IDENTIFICATION AND EGO DEVELOPMENT

Freud assumed that the id drives of sex and aggression require objects for their gratification and are, in turn, modified by the nature of those objects. If the object sought is no longer available, the ego offers the self to the drives as the object after attempting to make a part of the self resemble, as much as possible, the missing object. The clinical phenomena on which this formulation is based are principally those involving loss of relationships with people, either through death or separation. The mourner, it had been observed, tends to take on some of the characteristics of the lost person, thus identifying himself with him. Through this process of identification, the theory states, the mourner magically preserves the object internally by becoming like the lost object. But identifications can come about from causes other than loss. The child has a primary tendency, Freud postulated, to become like the significant adult models in his environment; during the oedipal phase of development, this tendency becomes an important vehicle for the solution of the oedipal conflict. One can observe the process of identification in the development of children in which the child tends to become like his parents in some respects.

Drives require objects for their expression; drives therefore press toward identification when objects are lost. But reality plays a role in identification in presenting an object or making the objects unavailable. The relationship with lost, unavailable, or renounced drive-objects shapes the ego through identifications, thereby giving it an identity and an individuality. There are, of course, instances in which incompatible identifications are made or in which identifications are not effectively integrated and reconciled with each other. These may result in pathological character formation.

MASTERY: FROM PASSIVITY TO ACTIVITY

The ego's tasks of drive modulation and reality attunement require the smooth operation of a number of psychological functions for the purpose of actively mastering stimuli from within and outside the organism. This function of mastery may represent another fundamental principle of human behavior: *the changing of a passive experience into an active one.* In Freud's words, "The ego develops from perceiving (drives) to controlling them [1933, p. 76]." In this task, reality-testing (distinguishing what is real from what is imaginary and illusory), consciousness, and the availability to consciousness of perceptions and memories are required. In becoming aware of these complex currents in development, psychoanalysis extended its interest into a study of these functions which, although incorporated into the early theory, could now be studied in their own right as ego functions.

The Superego

Several clinical observations prompted Freud to formulate the concept of the *superego*. First, there were the delusions of being observed as experienced by paranoid patients. It seemed to Freud that the content of these delusions (for example, the patient's conviction that others were constantly watching him to see if he looked at women) apparently stemmed from the patient's own self-scrutiny and self-criticism. Second, there was the high degree of self-criticism reported by obsessional patients during their psychoanalytic treatment. Both of these phenomena suggested the presence of a self-observing and self-criticizing function of the personality. A third fact that seemed relevant was the observation that self-regard could be enhanced by the experience of being loved by others and diminished or lessened by the experience of not being loved. In addition, Freud observed that self-esteem increased when one recognized desirable qualities in oneself and, conversely, that self-esteem decreased even to the point of shame (Piers & Singer, 1953) when one recognized undesirable qualities in oneself. All these observations suggested to Freud a separate set of functions which served to regulate behavior both through the conscience and through other inner imperatives. Such considerations required the concept of the superego.

We have mentioned that one way in which the ego grows and takes shape is by means of identifications. The child becomes like those who care for him, whether or not he loses a parent. Identifications may, of course, have consequences other than building and shaping the ego's character. Attitudes of the parents, including primitive, critical, and judgmental attitudes, are taken over by a child and become part of his inner world. Freud called these aspects of the child's ego the *superego*.

The origins of the superego, according to Freud, are to be traced to the oedipal phase of development, although Melanie Klein has suggested that many precursors could be discerned much earlier. According to Freud's theory, during the phallic phase, and especially at the height of the Oedipus complex, the child's sexual interests center upon the presence or absence of a phallus. During this period, the boy becomes an actively intruding being, thrusting himself into things, experiences, and relationships. This phase requires that the child give up his erotic attachment to the parent of the opposite sex. For the boy, the father's implied threats to harm or castrate him spur the renunciation. The boy responds by identifying himself both with his mother, whom he must give up as a libidinal object, and with his father. The maternal identifications color his character since, as in mourning, the object given up is reinstated in the self. The latter identifications include the "oughts and ought-nots" of the father as well as the fantasied cruelty and revenge. These injunctions became part of the superego by which the child judges himself.

Naturally contradictory identifications are formed. Because the father, although primarily a rival, is also regarded as a love object, the mother is the rival. The extent of the child's masculine or feminine identification and the character of his superego identifications reflect another of those complementary series discussed earlier (see page 124). This series refers to the relationship between the constitutional strength of the male-female elements of one's bisexuality and the impact of actual family experiences in the process of identification. As with other complementarities, the more one factor is present, the less the other is needed to bring about particular results—here the masculine or feminine characteristics. Likewise, sexual object choices, whether heterosexual or homosexual, can be understood with reference to this pattern of complementarity.

Once formed, the superego criticizes and judges harshly and imperiously. Because it is in contact with the drive-related wishes by being, as they are, dynamically unconscious, it can anticipate the activity of wishes of which it disapproves and can then exact painful feelings of guilt or acts of self-punishment. The superego can exact punishment for the continuing forbidden relationship with the mother (because the relationship has been continued through identification) causing unconscious guilt. Furthermore, since the child has become, through identification, similar to the feared parent or father, he can be hated and despised by the superego just as the father himself was. The child can even be reproached by the superego on the grounds that identifying with the parent is tantamount (in fantasy) to dispensing with or replacing him. Conflicts originally between the child and his parents thus become internal—an internalization which actually represents a progressive independence from the external world.

These dynamics of superego formation can be traced to Freud's earliest explanations of psychopathology in which he discussed conflicts involving the patient's ethical ideals. These ideals, after all, reflect parental training and values and are the standards by which a person gauges his self-respect. In his paper "On Narcissism: An Introduction," Freud (1914b) proposed that the setting up of an ego ideal was one way of regaining lost narcissism. With the formulation of the structural model in 1923, the ego ideal was included as an aspect of the superego. Both the superego and the ego ideal then became part of the ego concept, and under them were subsumed the special functions of self-observation, self-judgment, and conscience. In this new model, ego controls such as defenses were conceived of as set in motion, not only by the perception of danger, but also by moral consideration of one's own conduct judged by part of one's self, the superego. When those standards are met, self-love, pride, and self-respect follow. When they are violated, a range of feelings of self-hatred ensues including inferiority feelings, depressions, and guilt-provoked self-punishment. In an analysis of the superego concept, Schafer (1960) has called attention to two qualities of the superego in addition to its punishing activities: its loving and admiring, as well as its loved and admired, aspects; all of these aspects represent residues of parental care.

Anxiety

The phenomenon of anxiety early became a focus of Freud's interest because of its ubiquitous presence in neurotic conditions. He first attempted to explain anxiety in 1895 (1895b) in the context of a primitive libido theory. Even when he had revised his drive theory in 1915, he left the anxiety theory unchanged. Essentially in these early papers, he regarded anxiety as an affect which results from a transformation of the quantitative component of the libidinal impulse that has been blocked from gratification. The second theory of anxiety, which appeared in 1926 in the work "Inhibitions, Symptoms and Anxiety," was coordinated with the structural theory and was psychological rather than "hydrodynamic" in nature, as the first theory had been.

THE FIRST THEORY OF ANXIETY

The early theory of anxiety was based on the observation that a response to a real danger situation results in an experience of fear which is followed by some expedient action, either attack or defense. One sees an onrushing car, feels fear, and dashes to safety. Beyond a certain point, the greater the component of fear, the less effective is the action that follows. However, a certain minimum of fear, perhaps enough to act as an alerting signal, produces optimal self-preserving responses. A closer look at the experience of fear shows that it can be described as an affect: according to Freud, like any other affect, fear has a motor component and a feeling component. The motor component is represented by such bodily responses as dilated pupils, accelerated heart beat, and perspiration, all activities of the sympathetic and parasympathetic nervous systems. The feeling component can range from mild apprehension to panic.

Neurotic anxiety differs from fear in that it appears in the absence of any visible danger, and it can take several forms, two of which are most common. The first form is a general apprehensiveness or a feeling of impending tragedy or disaster ("free-floating anxiety"). The second form consists of anxieties which are more closely related to specific situations. These are called *phobias*. Some of these phobias which are extremely common may be at least partially understood as general, human, reflexive responses to potentially dangerous situations. The fear of snakes and spiders falls into this group. Other phobias, however, such as the fear of open spaces, do not appear to be rational. In these, as in the "free-floating anxieties," the relationship between anxiety and a real danger is not apparent. To explain the presence of anxiety in these situations, Freud made three observations:

1.   Anxiety appears if sexual gratification is interfered with, as in prolonged sexual privation or repetitive *coitus interruptus*. Freud had long assumed a relationship between anxiety and libido; many of his patients who complained of severe anxiety attacks also reported sexual frustrations. Many women patients, for example, complained that they never reached a satisfying sexual climax because they engaged in *coitus interruptus* or because their husbands suffered from premature ejaculations or other potency problems. Many men also complained of insufficient and inadequate sexual experiences.

2.   In psychoanalyses of patients suffering from hysteria, Freud noted that when repressions interfered with expressions of impulses, anxiety appeared in their place. For example, a young woman was able to repress impulses to murder her mother, but whenever she visited her mother, she felt such overpowering anxiety that she could stay only a few minutes.

3.   In phobias and obsessional rituals, anxiety appeared if the patient was forced to venture into the dreaded situation or was prevented from performing the compulsive ritual. For example, if one is

frightened of closed spaces (claustrophobia), it is only necessary for such a person to be in a closed room for paralyzing anxiety to develop.

Freud thus concluded that anxiety results from an interference with the expression of an impulse and that defensive mechanisms or symptoms resulting from the defenses appear secondarily and serve to protect the person from experiencing the anxiety. These conjectures and observations were then organized into a more formal restatement as a theory of anxiety: *Anxiety is the result of the transformation of the affect of a repressed impulse.* Other defensive measures are then required to bind the anxiety.

THE SECOND THEORY OF ANXIETY

The second, or structural, theory of anxiety, formulated in 1926, begins with the same clinical observations but weighs the structural factors differently. In this theory, libido is not assumed to be converted into anxiety. Freud had been dissatisfied with that formulation, for the process by which the transformation was to occur eluded rational explanation. Freud now placed the principal emphasis on the ego's role in sensing danger. A small quantity of anxiety acted as a signal to alert the organism, by means of the pleasure principle, to take appropriate and expedient defensive action (repression or other defensive behavior) against the threatened danger. Thus in the second anxiety theory, *repression results from anxiety rather than precedes it* (Freud, 1926).

But what was the nature of the danger situation in anxiety? Freud assumed that although no realistic danger might actually exist in the present, developmentally the organism had been faced with realistic dangers. He assumed that the ultimate danger to the organism had been that of helplessness, and he described a series of dangers appropriate to each developmental stage. Freud considered the birth situation to be the prototype of anxiety, for the massive motor response to the birth process—a danger situation imposed by a sudden new form of existence—seemed very much related to the affect of anxiety. Subsequent to birth, other situations of danger provoked anxiety. One of these dangers was the possibility of abandonment by the mother in early infancy; others were the possibility of castration by the father during oedipal struggles and, later, the possibility of punishment and "loss of love" from the superego. Although the danger common to this series is a reality-based helplessness through loss of love, the drives, by bringing the child into those reality situations, are incriminated in the danger. Thus drives become dangerous because of the possibility that they could lead to the reality dangers of loss of love or abandonment. Drives and reality are inextricably linked as sources of danger to the ego, external danger becoming dangerous because of the drives, and the drives becoming dangerous because of reality. The organism is vulnerable not only to being deserted and abandoned but also to the danger of being helpless by virtue of being overwhelmed by excessive stimulation. Reactions against being overwhelmed by the endogenous stimuli represented by the drives may be another source of danger and hence of anxiety.

In response to perceived danger, the ego, acting under the regulation of the pleasure principle, gives the signal of anxiety to itself and automatically sets in motion protective, defensive behaviors. This process is another example of the tendency of the organism to convert a passive experience into one actively reproduced. The organism can produce an anticipation of danger and an attenuated form of anxiety response to the danger situation. The ego can then actively cope with the attenuated anxiety by defensive behavior. A small, easily managed, "signal anxiety" replaces and symbolizes the massive anxiety.

The anxiety signal triggers repression of the offending ideas and then activates other defenses to maintain the repression and to prevent the continuation of the struggle with the drive. These defenses become fixed patterns of behavior which have a stability and persistence typical for each person and recognizable as part of his "character." An aggressive impulse, if repressed because of its dangerous implications, could be further defended by, for example, an altruistic stance. This altruistic behavior is itself a composite of many behaviors. In the defensive struggle, however, the external dangers are only internalized, not lost, and the conflict is thus continued.

One important implication of this second formulation of anxiety is the renewed role which social reality plays in the theory. In the 1890s, reality was the sole source of conflict. In the period from 1900 to 1928, perhaps because of Freud's awareness of his patients' distorted retrospective accounts of their lives, social reality played a wholly subordinate role to the struggle with the drives and their psychological representations. From the time of the publication of "The Ego and The Id" in 1923, and particularly of "Inhibitions, Symptoms and Anxiety" in 1926, reality entered the theory again insofar as it was implicated in the dynamics of the drives.

Summary

The structural model of psychoanalysis came into being as a response to a number of defects in the earlier models. The "structures" referred principally to two major systems: the id, the reservoir of the drives, and the ego, the organization of functions involved in control over drives and in adaptation to reality. As a result of the formulation of the structural model, a number of issues became part of the concerns of psychoanalysis. These included the ontogenetic development of ego functions such as perception and memory, the status of defensive strategies characteristic of particular persons, the issues of character, conscience, morality, and anxiety.

CHAPTER 10

THE WIDENING SCOPE

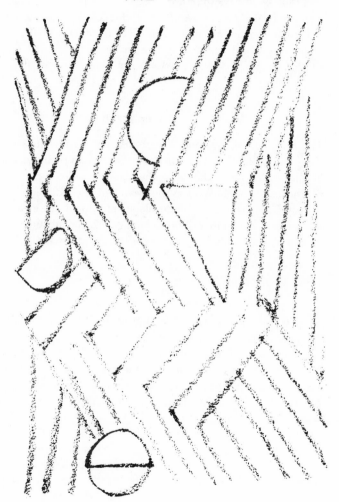

The introduction of the ego concept into psychoanalytic theory spurred psychoanalysts to study human experience beyond the confines of drive-dominated behavior. With the consideration of ego processes, psycho-analysis after 1926 became the general psychology that Freud had en-visaged in 1900. The environmental aspects of the theory, however, still remained relatively less developed than those concerned with drives and their control, despite some interesting attempts to build a psycho-analytically influenced sociology, anthropology, and history. Some of the major attempts in those areas will be mentioned briefly.

By way of introduction to this material, let us first discuss some of the work of a great practical contributor to our field of study: Anna Freud.

ANNA FREUD

The daughter of Sigmund Freud, sharing his lucidity, simplicity of style, and profundity, made her contributions to psychoanalytic theory in three areas: (1) clarifying the theory of defenses, (2) applying psychoanalytic techniques to the treatment of children and broadening the psychoanalytic theory of development through the method of direct observations of children, (3) developing tools and instruments to extract data derived from the psychoanalytic treatment situation.

The Theory of Defenses

After Freud's publication of "Inhibitions, Symptoms and Anxiety" in 1926, *depth psychology*, that is, the study of basic drives, was no longer the main focus of psychoanalysis. The central concern became the ex-ploration of the functions subsumed under the three major structures of id, ego, and superego, and the relationships of these structures to each other and to the environment. The functions of the ego, in particular, became a major interest, because the ego was recognized as the medium through which the influence of the drives and the restraints of the superego are apparent. The drives themselves did not appear directly in action. They were to be inferred from observed behavior which, it was assumed, had already been regulated by the ego. The effects of drive and superego pressures on the ego were still thought to be observed best during situations of conflict, particularly in internalized "neurotic conflict." Therefore neurotic patients in psychoanalytic treatment remained the principal group studied. The method of study was the psychoanalytic treatment situation. No experimentation was undertaken; rather, case studies were published and on the basis of those observations, new formulations were made about subjective experiences.

In 1936 Anna Freud published her book *The Ego and the Mechanisms of Defense* (revised edition: 1967) which continued the logical argument presented in Freud's 1926 work. In it she outlined a theory of defensive behavior which specified how, and against what, ego functions are recruited for defensive purposes. She argued that since some aspects of all three of the psychic structures—id, ego, and superego—are unconscious, analytic efforts must be directed towards bringing their unconscious aspects into awareness. In practice, when the analyst tries to do this, he typically meets with resistances which consist, in part, of the patient's typical defenses against the ideational manifestations of drives. They are, however, discernible also as defenses against affects. Some patients, for example, totally suppress or deny their emotions, being unaware or unable to admit that they are sad or angry or embarrassed.

Defensive patterns may become quite stable and rigid; they may even become divorced from their original role in a specific conflict and may take on the quality of those permanent character traits which Wilhelm Reich called "character armor." (Reich, 1949) Examples of these traits are such behaviors as a typically rigid posture, a perennial smile, or a haughty expression. Defensive behaviors thus become characteristic of a particular person.

DEFENSES AND CHOICE OF NEUROSIS

There is a relationship between the typical defenses employed by a person and the form of neurosis he will manifest, if he becomes ill. The psychoanalyst, from his vantage point of observer of the patient's expressed thoughts and life history, is able to see that the defenses the patient uses against free associating—the basic requirement of psychoanalytic treatment—are the same defenses that he employs against drives and that have resulted in symptom formation. For example, the hysterical patient who attempts to defend against her drives by repression of their ideational representations will also, during her attempts to free associate, demonstrate gaps in her awareness as manifested behaviorally by silence and subjectively as blankness. Her memory organization also will show gaps which make her appear to be naïve and unsophisticated, a person who throughout her life has shunned ideas in favor of feeling qualities. Therefore, her cultural and intellectual interests will be narrowed.

The obsessional patient, on the other hand, will employ isolation and reaction formation as typical defenses against drives. These devices permit the ideational representations of drives to remain conscious but unconnected to specific feelings or isolated from a wider context. Thus during free association, thoughts may flow freely but be linked with little feeling. Situations usually experienced as painful—for example, the death of a father—may be talked about with little feeling.

Anna Freud listed nine principal mechanisms of defense, all previously described by Freud: regression, repression, reaction formation, isolation, undoing, projection, introjection, turning against the self, and reversal.

Each of these represents a way of diverting drive representations from their original aims. Each has a special relation to particular forms of psychopathology. For example, repression is associated with hysteria; isolation, reaction formation, regression, and undoing are typical of obsessional neurosis; introjection and turning against the self are prominent in many depressions.

THE MOTIVES FOR DEFENSE

A person may fear the expression of drives for highly variable reasons. Anna Freud distinguished four main motives for defense against drives: (1) superego anxiety, (2) objective anxiety (in children), (3) anxiety about the strength of the drives, and (4) anxiety stemming from conflicts between mutually incompatible drives.

1. *Superego anxiety.* A person may be pressed into conflict with particular drives because of his ideals and standards, internalized prohibitions against the drives, and self-imposed demands for renunciation of them. Expression of his drives will represent a danger to the person, and their arousal will trigger anxiety. Some psychoanalysts have re-

garded this source of anxiety, and hence of defensive behavior and subsequent neurosis, as the sole source of neurosis and have concluded that managing and disposing of the superego may be a way of preventing neurosis. That is, conflict and neurosis may be prevented if in child-rearing, the creation of an excessively strict conscience can be avoided. Anna Freud, less optimistic, pointed out that this hope ignores the concept of the complementary series (see page 124) and the role of realistic anxiety in neurosis.

2. *Objective anxiety in childhood.* Children soon become aware that drive expression brings them into conflict with their parents and that to avoid the loss of their parents' love, they must renounce or curb some manifestations of their drives. Here defenses are motivated not by a conflict with internalized representation of the parents—the superego—but by a conflict with the parents themselves. It might be thought that by instructing parents to control their children without severity, violence, intimidation, and the resulting suppression of drives, psychoanalysts might be able to prevent the occurrence of neurosis. However, other factors would remain as potential bases for neurosis.

3. *Anxiety about the strength of drives.* The fear of being overwhelmed by excessive drive stimulation is ultimately a fear of total helplessness—a fear of being unable to act in one's own behalf or of being wholly at the mercy of a push from inner drives. Such situations can be observed in children who have experienced a minimum of superego anxiety and objective anxiety because of careful rearing or whose anxieties have been removed through successful psychoanalytic intervention. Such children may show a striking fear of their own aggressive or sexual impulses.

> In later life we can see it in full force whenever a sudden accession of instinctual energy threatens to upset the balance of the psychic institutions, as is normally the case, owing to physiological changes, at puberty and the climacteric [Freud, A., 1967, p. 64].

4. *Anxiety stemming from conflicts between mutually incompatible aims.* The fourth motive of defense is that triggered by experiences of disharmony and dissonance within the person. Contrary tendencies stemming from biological pressures—for example, heterosexuality versus homosexuality—provoke defensive responses. A person may feel compelled to defend himself against one or both of these competing or contradictory urges. For example, in the instance of the simultaneous urges to homosexuality and heterosexuality, a man may exaggerate his masculinity to the extent that he acts like a Don Juan, becoming totally absorbed in making conquests of women.

The Technique of Child Psychoanalysis

The second psychoanalytic advance which Anna Freud helped to produce was to develop psychoanalytic techniques applicable to children. Because of their limited capacity for verbalization, children cannot follow the basic rule of psychoanalysis with adults—free association. Alternative techniques for children that make use of play and other activities have become an integral part of the repertoire for the treatment of children. These techniques owe their development to Anna Freud whose first lecture on the technique of child analysis appeared in 1926. Other workers had made significant contributions to this sphere as well. In 1908 Freud himself had supervised the treatment conducted by the father of a five-year-old boy who suffered from a horse phobia (Freud, 1909). Melanie Klein, who contributed greatly to the application of psychoanalytic techniques to children, had begun to treat children with psychoanalysis in 1919 (Klein, M., 1963). The extension of psychoanalytic treatment principles to children opened the door to many observations of child development and child psychopathology.

The Broadening of the Psychoanalytic Theory of Development through Direct Observations of Children

Anna Freud's direct and extensive experience with children— she was a teacher before she became a psychoanalyst—gave her access to observations about child development not available to analysts of adult patients. Her observations permitted her to make a further extension of psychoanalysis into normal psychology. She developed the concept of *developmental lines* (Freud, A., 1963) in which she proposed a schedule of development of several important sexual, aggressive, and social strands or lines from infancy through latency. In general, the lines trace the child's growth from his early dependence on environmental supports and id motivations to his relative autonomy from both. Conflicts, traumas, and unusual circumstances can affect the progress along one or more developmental lines.

FROM DEPENDENCY TO SELF-RELIANCE

One developmental line described most fully deals with the child's progress from dependency to emotional self-reliance and adult object-relationships. She distinguishes eight phases in this developmental line: (1) the phase of the biological unity of mother and infant in which experiences of separations and individuality are not yet significant features of the infant's inner life; (2) the phase in which the relationship with the mother is motivated by the appearance of a child's needs; (3) the phase of forming permanent representations of others whether or not needs are gratified; (4) the phase of ambivalent relationships to significant adults—a clinging, teasing, and controlling phase; (5) the phase of oedipal possessiveness and rivalry; (6) the phase of loosening ties to the parents, including a growing disillusionment with them while forming strong friendships, ideals, and interests; (7) the phase of preadolescent need-dominated relationships; and (8) the phase of adolescent separations from the parents while beginning to form mature heterosexual relationships.

Another developmental line traces eating behavior from sucking to rational eating. It encompasses the progress of the child's regulation of his food intake from being nursed to being weaned to self-feeding; later, the child becomes relatively independent of the mother and, still later, develops first partly irrational and then, finally, rational attitudes toward food and eating. Still another line extends from irresponsibility to responsibility in body management.

The concept of the developmental lines has its chief value in setting forth an expected sequence of normal development. Since correspondences between several lines can be followed, irregularities in growth can be spotted. These irregularities may represent variations of normal growth or pathological discontinuities. An integration of this concept with Erikson's psychosocial epigenesis, to be described below, would certainly be extremely valuable.

Psychoanalytic Research

A third major contribution of Anna Freud has been a research attempt to standardize the storage, retrieval, and reporting of psychoanalytic data, particularly clinical data.

In her project the 90 to 100 child patients seen in psychoanalytic treatment each year in her Hampstead Clinic in London, as well as non-patient children enrolled in the nursery school operated by the Clinic, have been studied. The Clinic patients present a range of psychopathological problems that include neuroses, character disorders, developmental disturbances, and severe sensory limitations. Miss Freud devised two research instruments to filter the vast amount of data accumulated through observations of the patients and the normal children: the Developmental Profile and the Hampstead Index.

THE DEVELOPMENTAL PROFILE

The developmental profile of a patient provides a method for organizing the examinational data so that different aspects can be seen in relation to each other. In particular, the relationship of pathology to normal functioning is studied. The profile is not an outline for carrying out a psychiatric examination; however, it is a way of formulating the case, with a focus on dynamic, genetic, adaptive, and structural factors and on the influence of the environmental forces. Profiles can be constructed before, during, or after treatment, and assumptions about the case can be confirmed or refuted by using proper safeguards for reliability of data and examiner judgment. A large pool of profiles about child cases has been accumulated which has facilitated the making of generalizations about conflicts, defenses, and dangers typical of the normal child at any given age. Some examples of completed profiles are in "Metapsychological Assessment of the Adult Personality: The Adult Profile" (Freud, A., Nagera, H., & Freud, W. E., 1965). In the profile, attention is focused on nonmotivational, as well as motivational, aspects of development; for example, the making of a profile requires statements about the child's frustration tolerance, capacity to delay action, and adaptive coping devices. The important role of these nonmotivational aspects in psychopathology became clear when a study of the case profiles revealed that some children do remarkably well and others poorly in the face of equal kinds of environmental frustrations and possibly even drive similarities. Thus, whether a child develops neurotic symptoms cannot be explained merely on the basis of the intensity of his drives, his conflicts with his parents, or his internalized conflicts. It depends as much on the capacities of the child to handle frustration and delay action and on his resilience in the face of adversity. These capacities are essentially those which Hartmann wrote about as "conflict-free" functions of the ego (see page 157).

THE INDEX

The index was devised by Dorothy Burlingame, a close co-worker of Anna Freud, as a simple guide for locating events in the case material and therapy notes. The investigators discerned very quickly that there was difficulty in determining the relationship between concrete events and abstract concepts like defenses or particular defenses like denial or drive characteristics such as anal aggression. Hence, in addition to its original purpose of enlarging the organized memory of psychoanalytic practice, the index took on the function of clarifying the concepts actually used. Several workers at the Hampstead Clinic have made use of the index in writing a number of concept clarifying papers—for example, Sandler's papers on the representational world (Sandler & Rosenblatt, 1962), on unconscious fantasy (Sandler & Nagera, 1963), and on the superego (Sandler, 1960).

Both the index and the profile became important additions to clinical assessment procedures and aids to the standardization of psychoanalytic terms, assertions, and concepts.

Several sources of conflict which may contribute to childhood and adult psychopathology have been empirically distinguished. These distinctions are of considerable clinical value. One of Anna Freud's co-workers, Nagera, has described three classes of conflict which are to be distinguished from neuroses:

1. *Developmental Interferences.* The environment may at times interfere with basic needs, and such interferences may create an excessive load on the child. Examples include food deprivation result-

ing in malnutrition, too rigid or too lenient toilet training, and absence of sufficient intensity and variety of sensory stimulation. Symptoms arising from such environmental interferences may appear to be similar to neurotic symptoms, but careful observation shows that they are not the outcome of conflict between drives and control, with a subsequent compromise. Therapeutic intervention will not be the same for these symptoms as for symptoms arising from neurotic conflicts.

2. *Developmental Conflicts.* These conflicts are distinguished from developmental interferences. They refer to inevitable conflicts of the child with care-providing people during the behavioral changes brought about by maturation, as during transitional periods such as weaning or toilet training. These conflicts apparently disappear when the child enters a new maturational phase.

3. *Neurotic Conflicts.* To be distinguished from "neuroses," which refer to an organized syndrome, neurotic conflicts refer to those developmental conflicts that persist even when the child enters a new developmental phase. They, therefore, denote an internalized struggle.

Each of these classes of conflicts may play a significant role in subsequent psychopathology, although their effect is dependent upon multiple determinants outlined in previous chapters.

HEINZ HARTMANN

In 1939 Heinz Hartmann published a monograph called *Ego Psychology and the Problem of Adaptation* (Hartmann, 1958). This work expands the ego theory that Freud developed in "Inhibitions, Symptoms and Anxiety," thrusting psychoanalysis firmly into the area of general psychology and moving it to the threshold of both sociology and the theory of evolution. His study of ego functions focused on relationships of the ego to reality, to other people, and to the social milieu. The ideas presented in his monograph were developed and expanded in a series of later papers by Hartmann (e.g., Hartmann, 1950) and also in other papers written in collaboration with Ernst Kris and Rudolph Loewenstein (e.g., Hartmann, H., Kris, E., & Loewenstein, R., 1946).

Adaptation

Studies of the human being in conflict show that conflict resolution relies upon many psychological functions that do not necessarily have their origin in conflict. For example, speech, motility, and learning employed in resolving conflicts are at least initially "conflict free." Hartmann set himself the task of investigating the interrelations of processes whose origins can be traced to conflicts and those whose origins cannot. One of his first premises is that the organism at birth is adapted to an *average expectable environment* and thereafter continues to adapt. This adaptation is guaranteed both by inborn biological and psychological apparatus and by the progressive maturation of those apparatus as they respond favorably to changes or disturbances in the environment. Thus Hartmann proposed that the newborn is not solely a "creature of drives" but at birth possesses functioning systems like perception and memory which are later refined and referred to as *ego functions*. In Hartmann's language, these functions ensure that "a state of adaptiveness exists before the intentional processes of adaptation begin [Hartmann, 1958, p. 49]."

Adaptation may come about by three means:

1. The changes the organism makes in the environment (alloplasticity)
2. The changes made in the organism by the environment (autoplasticity)
3. Removal of the organism from one environment to another

In the first two means of adaptation—alloplastic and autoplastic—a reciprocal relationship is implied between organism and environment, for in changing the environment, the human being ultimately changes himself in adapting to his newly created environment. The ego is thus seen by Hartmann as not merely the outcome of the taming of the drives by reality. The ego has an origin independent of the conflict between drives and reality.

The Origins of Ego Development

Hartmann distinguished three origins of the development of ego functions: (1) inherited or autonomous functions, (2) effects of drive requirements, and (3) effects of reality frustrations. None of the three is a sufficient condition for the development of ego functions. In addition, Hartmann explicitly recognized the important role of reality in ego development. According to Hartmann, the organism is innately adapted to an "average expectable" reality, and with the unfolding maturation of the organism, reality presents a series of new "average expectable environments" which calls for a series of new adaptations.

The Concept of Reality

In Hartmann's view, reality enters the psychoanalytic theory as more than a source of conflict, of frustration, or of gratification of drives. Hartmann explains man's relation to his environment not solely in terms of the requirements of the self-preservative drives of the early psychoanalytic model. Man's purpose must not be merely to conform to the environment; indeed, there are circumstances in which such conformity would not be adaptive. He has the task of actively molding the environment to which he adapts. In Hartmann's words:

> From the very beginning of life . . . man adapts to an environment part of which has not, but part of which has already been molded by his kind and himself. Man not only adapts to the community but also actively participates in creating the conditions to which he must adapt. Man's environment is molded increasingly by man himself. Thus the crucial adaptation man has to make is to the social structure and his collaboration in building it [1958, p. 31].

This view represents a shift from a narrow view of psychic structure limited to clinical-pathological phenomena—such as resistances and defenses—to a broader biological view of man in his environment.

Primary Autonomy and the Conflict-free Sphere

From this initial orientation, Hartmann developed several propositions. Ego and drive functions are presumed to differentiate from an undifferentiated matrix. Further, certain psychological structures—those involved in perception, memory, and learning, as well as inhibition—are at least partly inborn and do not develop solely from the impact of inner needs or of reality. Their maturation follows certain laws which are part of biological inheritance, although the specific ways in which these apparatus function reflect learning and the impact of reality. Because they have an "autonomous developmental course," in Hartmann's language, and seem to be mainly independent of drive factors in their origin, Hartmann called them ego apparatus of *primary autonomy*. In the course of development, however, the functioning of these apparatus may become embroiled in a neurotic conflict. They may then be required to mediate between drives and the defensive counterforces. Learning, perception, motility, and other primary autonomous functions can thus bear the marks of conflict, as, for example, in learning blocks, psychogenic perceptual distortions, and hysterical paralyses. For the most part, however, these apparatus and their contents function independently of conflict, as a *conflict-free sphere* of the ego.

Secondary Autonomy

Certain functions which have been spawned from drive pressures and from conflict can attain a relative autonomy from their sources by becoming part of the conflict-free sphere and can achieve what Hartmann called a *secondary autonomy*. This concept is analogous to Gordon Allport's concept of *functional autonomy* and to Gardner Murphy's concept of *canalization* (Murphy, 1966). Allport used the term "functional autonomy" (Allport, 1937) to describe action patterns which at a former time satisfied basic drives but which have become satisfying in their own right. Murphy's concept of "canalization" refers to the progressive learning of ways of satisfying drives. Familiar objects tend to be more and more liked; a hungry man searches for familiar foods and avoids strange ones. Soon these canalized objects may themselves be sources of pleasure, perhaps even relatively greater than the pleasure related to the motives they originally served. Thus an attitude that originally had served a defensive purpose may achieve an existence that is independent of its original pupose and may serve in nonconflict areas. For example, a forty-year-old man defended himself against strong urges to acquire other people's property by becoming altruistic. His acquisitiveness had its origin when, after a sibling was born, he had to give up his central place in his family. He resented having to share his toys and his parents. But he quickly learned that it was "bad" to express his anger, annoyance, and unbridled grasping. In place of the acquisitiveness there appeared its opposite, an altruism and generosity that won back for him the lost affection and status. Later in life, when the original conflicts that provoked his reactive altruism were no longer relevant, the altruism nevertheless persisted. Although it no longer served its original purposes, it continued to be a source of intrinsic gratification, for this man truly enjoyed sharing and helping. The process by which a secondary autonomy is achieved is called by Hartmann *change of function*. Thus Hartmann's views separate the concepts of genesis (the origins of an apparatus) and of function (the use made of the apparatus).

Defenses, like other ego functions, have diverse origins:

1. Defenses may be modeled after some form of drive behavior. For example, in the defense of "introjection" the representation of a significant other person is taken in, with the result that communication with some aspect of that other person can be carried on. Many times this process serves defensive purposes; thus, one psychotic patient carried on hostile battles with the "introject" of his father but was able to maintain cordial and even warm relations with his actual father and thus defend himself against an actual clash. In less extreme forms of introjection, the other person is felt to be with one, around one, or within one. The process of introjection would appear to be modeled after the drive toward oral incorporation.

2. Other defenses may be based on specific characteristics of the primary process. "Displacement," for example, refers to the removal of intensity or interest from one idea for investment in another (see page 101); it can be used defensively, as when a man who is afraid of sexually forward women develops a cat phobia.

3.   Defenses may be modeled after an autonomous ego function; attention used in the mechanism of isolation is an example. Isolation permits a person to separate many potentially anxiety-provoking ideas from their concomitant, unpleasant affect and to keep separate two ideas which, if related to each other, would arouse anxiety. Freud proposed that isolation of idea from affect and of idea from idea came about from intense attention and concentration upon the ideas. Thus, defensive isolation operates through the particular deployment of the autonomous ego function of concentration and attention.

4.   The prototype of a defense may be a reflexive defense against outside stimuli. An example is the eye blink as the prototype of the defense of avoidance, that is, the deliberate avoidance of dangerous situations. Anna Freud described the following example of avoidance:

When I was analyzing [a little boy], I was able to observe how his avoidance of "pain" developed on these lines. One day when he was at my house, he found a little magic drawing-block which appealed to him greatly. He began enthusiastically to rub the pages, one by one, with a colored pencil and was pleased when I did the same. Suddenly, however, he glanced at what I was doing, came to a stop and was evidently upset. The next moment he put down his pencil, pushed the whole apparatus (hitherto jealously guarded) across to me, stood up and said, "you go on doing it; I would much rather watch." Obviously when he looked at my drawing it struck him as more beautiful, more skillful, somehow more perfect than his own and decided that he would not compete with me any more, since the results were disagreeable and thereupon he abandoned the activity which, a moment ago, had given him pleasure. He adopted the role of the spectator who does nothing and so cannot have his performance compared with that of someone else. By imposing this restriction on himself the child avoided a repetition of a disagreeable impression [Freud, A., 1967, pp. 100–101].

Ego Motives

Hartmann also turned his attention to those drive qualities which Freud, in his early drive theory, called the self-preservative drives.

This group of tendencies which comprises strivings for what is "useful," egoism, self-assertion, etc., should, it seems reasonable, be attributed to the system ego. The importance of these tendencies has been somewhat neglected in analysis, probably because they play no essential part in the etiology of neurosis and because in work with patients we have to consider them more from the angle of genetically id tendencies than in their partly independent aspects as functions of the ego. But the relevance of this latter aspect becomes obvious the moment we turn to viewing them from the angle of general psychology [Hartmann, 1950, p. 135].[1]

ERIK ERIKSON

Erikson's Psychosocial Theory

The development of ego processes in relation to drives and reality is the theme of Erik Erikson's writings. Whereas Freud postulated the endogenous unfolding of the sexual and aggressive drives and described in some detail their manifestations through adolescence, Erikson provided for this development a theoretical setting that fuses psychological, social, and biological factors into a unity and describes drive development as continuing past childhood and adolescence and through three stages of adulthood. His data, like Freud's, came from psychoanalytic treatment of children and adults, from observations of children in other than therapeutic situations, from anthropological data (Erikson, 1963) and from a study of the biographies of unusual people such as Gorky (Erikson, 1963), Hitler (Erikson, 1963), Luther (Erikson, 1958), and Gandhi (Erikson, 1968). From these data, and within the psychoanalytic ego theory, he reconstructed presumed stages of development. The stages are not linear but proceed in leaps according to an epigenetic process.

Epigenesis

Epigenesis is a term borrowed from embryology. It refers to the predetermined sequential development of parts of an organism. Each of the parts has a special time for its emergence and for its progressive integration within the functioning whole. Each phase of emergence depends upon the successful completion of the preceding phase. Thus environmental forces have a greater influence on development at the earliest

[1] This aspect of psychoanalytic theory has been elaborated by White in his theory of effectance motivation, although White's emphasis would replace all drives by the ego motivations (White, 1963).

stages of growth, because anything that disturbs one stage will affect all subsequent stages dependent upon it. As if according to a biological timetable, a given stage must be superseded by a new one, receding in significance as the new assumes dominance. A constant cogwheeling at critical periods of the emergence of some parts and the suppression of others must proceed smoothly lest excesses or defects of development appear.

Erikson distinguished two lines of epigenetic growth: psychosexual and psychosocial.

Psychosexual Epigenesis

In psychoanalytic writings, the sexual drive was described, not as emerging in its final genital form, but rather as developing epigenetically with the emergence of the oral, anal, phallic, and genital phases. Erikson added to this two phases—puberty and adulthood—and thus extended the psychoanalytic theory of drives and development through adulthood. To the sequence of phases of sexual drive development he added a sequence of *modes,* that is, forms through which drives manifest themselves. In the first oral stage the mode is *incorporation,* and it is seen in the predominant activities of receiving and accepting what is presented. The child's receptiveness is expressed not merely with his mouth but with other functional systems such as the sense organs. In the second oral stage the mode is *taking things,* whether edible or inedible. In the first anal phase, *letting-go* is the mode, and in the second anal stage it is that of *retaining* or holding on to one's own or other products. The phallic phase is expressed through the mode of intrusiveness into people or things. In the development of the girl the mode that becomes characteristic of genitality is *inceptiveness,* that of including and enveloping within. These modes are ways of expressing drives in thought and action. In the course of development, a particular mode tends to appear during the specific time a particular zone is becoming dominant. Thus, when the mouth is the dominant zone, incorporation and taking in appear as modes. The modes, however, may become independent of the zone and persist either to influence the function of zones that become dominant at a later time or as determinants of particular styles of character.

Society's Modalities

The appearance of a mode is shaped and reinforced by the surrounding society which, with its own *modalities*, meets the expressions of the mode. Societal modalities differ from culture to culture. There is a reciprocal interaction of the mode and modality, each new mode as it appears being met by the available societal modality.

In some societies, a young infant is kept swaddled for its first year to protect him from harming himself; in others, he is allowed free motion but is required to plead (to the extent of becoming blue in the face) for his needs. There is thus a spectrum of societal ways of handling a mode; the "average expectable environment" varies from culture to culture. The interaction of individual mode and societal modality creates what is sometimes called *psychosocial* or *ego epigenesis*.

Psychosocial Epigenesis

The infant's experiences, which are functions of the interaction of drive and environmental supports (e.g., social modalities), leave their residue in a series of polar attitudes towards himself and the world. Erikson described these polar attitudes for eight stages of development:

1. *Basic Trust versus Mistrust*. This phase is associated with the oral-receptive stage. The infant's mothering experience provides the principal contouring of his sense of basic trust or mistrust.
2. *Autonomy versus Shame and Doubt*. The second stage arises in association with the child's critical attempts to control and coordinate, not just anal functions, but other striated muscle systems and to tame them to his own will and desires. Success in this phase leads to self-expression, failure to shame and doubt.
3. *Initiative versus Guilt*. The third stage has its period of ascendance in association with the progressive mastery over locomotion and of language; the danger of this phase is a sense of guilt over the mastery, manipulation, and aggression implied by success.
4. *Industry versus Inferiority*. The fourth stage arises in early latency and is associated with the opportunity to master or fail to master the skills of tool use.

5. *Identity versus Identity Confusion*. The fifth stage, that of identity formation, has been most extensively studied by Erikson. It marks the integration at puberty of the earlier experiences that give the child a sense that he is a person with a history, a stability, and a continuity that is recognizable by others. The establishing of a personal identity requires the selective arrangement of previous identifications with significant others. It calls for the abandonment or suppression of some identifications and the preserving of others. Unsuccessful identity formation results in *identity confusion,* a term which describes an inability to set a direction for oneself on the basis of one's self-representations. It manifests itself in scattered work habits, concentration difficulties, problems in forming close and stable friendships with appropriate partners, and a feeling of despair about establishing oneself in life. Identity confusion can be mild or severe, acute or long-lasting.

Erikson then extended his scheme by describing three stages of adulthood, representing the sixth, seventh, and eighth psychosocial stages of man.

6. *Intimacy and Distantiation versus Self-Absorption*. This phase is characteristic of early adult life. Intimacy refers not only to the capacity for mature genital relations with a loved partner of the opposite sex but also to the capacity to form and maintain friendships and interests. Distantiation refers to the ability to abandon or fight against or otherwise take distance from noxious situations. Self-absorption means a failure to establish the ascendance of intimacy, thus permitting a regressive retreat to exclusive concern with oneself.

7. *Generativity versus Stagnation*. This phase is concerned with activities that establish and guide the next generation by sexual procreation and by teaching skills, cultural expectations, and social responsibilities.

8. *Integrity versus Despair and Disgust*. Erikson writes that integrity implies acceptance of oneself and others, even given their shortcomings, and an acceptance of responsibility, whereas despair and disgust imply dissatisfaction with one's accomplishments, often manifested by disgust with others.

These stages describe the psychosocial advances expected in healthy personality growth and the possible harmful detours along the route. Regressions to previous stages or the persistence of earlier stages are also represented in the scheme as psychopathological. Erikson's theoretical contributions are loosely stated in a number of papers. The richness of his ideas lies in the integration of the theories of drives, ego, and social forces, and in the references to phenomenological data.

Other Developments

The impact of the ego psychological movement was not confined to psychoanalysis. Large segments of general psychology were affected, as the works of David Rapaport and George Klein bear witness.

David Rapaport was chiefly responsible for developing diagnostic psychological testing into a finely honed tool that permitted the psychologist to assess more than the mere intelligence level of a patient. His stress was on the forms and styles of thinking characteristic of a patient. Through a study of test responses, which included the answer to a test question and the way in which the answer was verbalized, it became possible to assess the patient's thought functions and to make inferences about the structures through which those functions are expressed. For example, the psychological-test diagnostician will assess whether, in response to a test question, a patient is relying upon attention, concentration, memory; he will further assess what motivational factors may be interfering with these functions and how adequately the patient is able to maintain his functional integrity. Psychological testing was pursued not to classify a patient into one or another specifically "diagnostic" rubric but to study the patient's characteristic thought organization and style of thinking which, when affected by pathology, showed recognizable varieties in content and form. Rapaport's work in diagnostic testing, undertaken with the collaboration of Roy Schafer and Merton Gill, (Rapaport, Schafer & Gill, 1968) and his subsequent contributions to psychoanalytic theory are rooted solidly within the ego psychology of Freud's later works beginning with "Inhibitions, Symptoms and Anxiety," and of the work of Hartmann and of Erikson (Rapaport, 1967). In his role as a psychoanalytic theorist, he developed the theory of ego functions that became relatively independent of drive motivations and environmental pressures. Toward the end of his life he confronted two major research issues: to study the various cognitive organizations that accompany different states of consciousness and to construct a psychoanalytic theory of learning.

George S. Klein, with his co-workers and students, studied individual consistencies in cognitive and perceptual behavior. He called those consistencies *cognitive controls* and called the patterning of various cognitive controls within a person *cognitive style* (Gardner, Holzman, Klein, Linton, & Spence, 1959). The study of these dimensions of perceptual and cognitive behavior has been chiefly confined to the psychological laboratory with normal subjects rather than in the psychoanalytic consulting room. The basic data are responses to various size-estimation tests, to illusions of apparent movement, and to memory tasks. The study of cognitive controls emphasizes the organism's internal psychological structures that guide adaptive efforts. It thus represents a study of conflict-free ego structures.

Klein has made empirical and theoretical contributions to the psychology of consciousness (Klein, 1959). He has elaborated Freud's early view of consciousness as an attention-deploying function of the ego system. The patterns of deployment determine the varieties of awareness of a stimulus, whether percept or memory. Thus consciousness, in Klein's view, is to be identified only with awareness of inner events as well as events in the environment. Klein's work addresses itself to the variety of ways in which an encounter with the environment or internal events can become conscious, to the many patterns of awareness possible, and to the organization of motives, intentions, and stimuli that influence experience. Klein and his co-workers have performed a number of experimental studies of stimulus reception under altered states of consciousness, such as sleep and reverie. The results of some of these studies bear upon a psychoanalytic theory of perception.

Summary

The introduction of the ego concept broadened psychoanalysis into a general psychology. Anna Freud studied the defensive process and examined the motives for defensive behavior. She also contributed to the development of psychoanalytic treatment techniques that are applicable to children and thus extended the observational field of psychoanalysis. New research methods based upon controlled observation were devised. Hartmann widened the environmental and biological concerns of psychoanalysis in his treatment of the theory of adaptation and of ego development independent of conflict. Erikson broadened the developmental theory by linking it to the concept of epigenesis and by extending psychosexual and psychosocial developmental considerations past childhood through three stages of adulthood.

CHAPTER 11

PSYCHOANALYSIS AND
PSYCHOPATHOLOGY

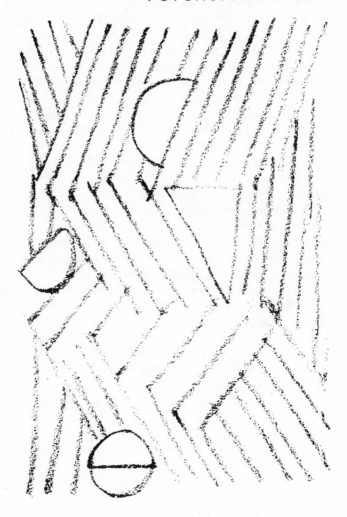

Retrospect

A SUMMARY

This book has surveyed Freud's psychoanalytic theories and models. We chose a historical rather than a systematic presentation because a number of difficulties inherent in the theory suggested to us, as it did to others (e.g., Rapaport, 1960), that a systematic view may be premature. We began with an overview of the spirit of the times during which Freud developed his theory, and we recorded the forces that restricted and limited Freud's conceptualizations as well as those that pushed him towards innovation. We then discussed the primary data which formed the basis of Freud's early theorizing and model-building. These data were the verbal reports of patients whose psychopathology Freud classified as "defense neuropsychoses." We contrasted the traditional psychiatric approaches to these patients with Freud's and examined the fundamental assumptions that directed Freud's approach: the assumptions (1) of defensive behavior and, therefore, of conflict, (2) of determinism, and (3) of unconscious psychological processes.

We then traced Freud's revisions in his formulations as he was confronted with contradictory evidence that came not only from a widening sample of patients but also from his own introspections. These revisions included the postulation of a drive theory as a necessary component of motivated behavior and of conflict. His study of the maturation of basic drives, but particularly of the sexual drive, underscored the importance of a person's past history as a determining condition of behavior, whether normal or pathological. Freud believed that genetic factors were not sufficient conditions for explaining behavior. He thought that all six metapsychological points of view—topographic, dynamic, structural, economic, genetic, and adaptive—were necessary for an understanding of behavior.

In presenting the history of the theory, we detoured from considerations of psychopathology to the study of "normal" psychological phenomena—slips, errors, and dreams—phenomena which Freud called the *psychopathology of everday life*. Close examination of these experiences permitted us to outline the highly complex model and theoretical formulations of mental functioning that Freud evolved. Much of that model remains the keystone of psychoanalytic thought. A closer look at the drive theory in its several versions followed. We then described Freud's final revisions of his theory which emphasized the structure of the mind and concluded with a survey of some recent additions to the psychoanalytic corpus.

The changing models and the basic method of psychoanalysis. Our survey has emphasized the progressive elaborations of and amendments to the theories and the models as more data entered the realm of psychoanalytic concerns. Within psychoanalytic circles there is a certain tolerance for looseness and inexactness in the construction of models. While such flexibility may be disquieting to some personality theorists, it is not at all undesirable, for models, unlike theories, are "as if" formulations which are expected to be inexact and inaccurate in some respects. Models can even remain in the presence of some contrary evidence (Chapanis, 1961).

Observational data shaped psychoanalytic ideas. But these data were not available to any casual observer. They were gathered through the use of a unique method, one available in no other psychological laboratory: that of free association within a therapeutic context. Free association gave psychoanalysts access to the inner life of their patients, to the content of people's minds which could not be fathomed by other psychological methods, such as that of questionnaire inventories, observations of behavior, or psychophysiological instrumentation. Today, too, it is principally through the free-association method that the psychoanalyst can glimpse ordinarily unconscious ideas and fantasies, such as archaic hates and loves, masturbatory or destructive urges, bizarre wishes, mysterious anxieties. A full appreciation of these phenomena requires a full instruction in and experience with the method.

Psychopathology

Our survey of psychoanalysis has, seemingly but not actually, taken us some distance from psychopathology. For, primarily, psychoanalysis brings to bear on psychopathology a point of view that stresses the continuity between the pathological and the nonpathological. Here is Freud's final statement on this issue.

The neuroses (unlike infectious diseases, for instance) have no specific determinants. It would be idle to seek in them for pathogenic excitants. They shade off by easy transitions into what is described as the normal; and, on the other hand, there is scarcely any state recognized as normal in which indications of neurotic traits could not be pointed out. Neurotics have approximately the same innate dispositions as other people, they have the same experiences and they have the same tasks to perform. Why is it, then, that they live so much worse and with so much greater difficulty and in the process suffer more feelings of unpleasure, anxiety, and pain?

We need not be at a loss to find an answer to this question. Quantitative disharmonies are what must be held responsible for the inadequacy and sufferings of neurotics. The determining cause of all the forms taken by human mental life is, indeed, to be sought in the reciprocal action between innate dispositions and accidental experiences. Now a particular instinct may be too strong or too weak innately, or a particular capacity may be stunted or insufficiently developed in life. On the other hand, external impressions and experiences may make demands of differing strength on different people; and what one person's constitution can deal with may prove an unmanageable task for another's. These quantitative differences will determine the variety of the results [Freud, 1940, pp. 183–184].

THE DISEASE MODEL

This point of view differs from those approaches to psychopathology which emphasize a search for specific causal agents, noxious invaders which can be exorcized, excised, or eradicated. In the middle-ages, the causal agent was thought to be an invasion of the individual by angels, God, devils, witches, or demons. Later, in 1563, in an only slightly more enlightened era, Johann Weyer considered that those people who behaved strangely were physically ill (Weyer, 1563). Thus, diseases were named as the invaders in place of the angels and devils. About 200 years later, the physician William Cullen coined the term "neurosis" and used it to refer to his conviction that strange behavior or mental aberrations reflected a malfunctioning of the nervous system (Cullen, 1772). The extreme form of this view was represented in the teachings of the German psychiatrist Griesinger who declared flatly that mental diseases were nothing but brain disease (Griesinger, 1867). A modern version of this point of view is contained in the writings of Percival Bailey (Bailey, 1956–1957). This view of psychopathology separates the disease from the person afflicted and thus regards the patient as one who has been invaded—without his complicity—whether by demons or by bacteria

(Reise, 1945). Because the conception of psychopathology was rooted in the traditions of a disease model, it is easy to understand why the activity of most psychiatrists was centered on classifying and naming the manifestations of illnesses. An excellent history and critique of this trend in medicine, and particularly in psychiatry, is contained in Karl Menninger's *The Vital Balance* (Menninger, Mayman, & Pruyser, 1963).

In contrast to this trend, the emphasis of psychoanalysis is not on the naming of psychopathological conditions—where there is a dubious kind of precision implied—but on trying to understand the patient. This person-centered focus in psychoanalysis emerged gradually. Freud's earliest attempts, it is true, were in the traditions of classical psychiatry, for some of his efforts went into describing specific etiologies and dynamics of various clinical syndromes (e.g., Freud, 1895a). There was, however, a significant difference between Freud's approach to psychopathology and that of the classical psychiatrists: Although he was interested in distinguishing "actual" from "defense" neuroses, "neurasthenia" from "anxiety neurosis" (e.g., Freud, 1895a), his principal effort was to search for the psychological meaning of the symptoms. He used diagnostic names like "hysteria" and "obsessional neurosis" as guides both to the treatability of the patient and to the reconstruction of earlier psychologically significant experiences in the patient's life.

Clinical psychoanalytic studies have always aimed at outlining a set of specific dynamics for psychopathological conditions. Insofar as these studies assumed the reality of entities like "hysteria" or "compulsion neurosis," they are, in the tradition of modern medicine, disease models of psychopathology. But the major focus of psychoanalytic psychopathology is on the understanding of the suffering person, an understanding that has been called *psychodynamics*.

PSYCHODYNAMICS

The most complete attempt to systematize psychoanalytic conceptions about psychopathological syndromes is that of Otto Fenichel (1945). Fenichel's work was encyclopedic; it gathered together in a scholarly manner all relevant psychoanalytic thought on the neuroses, psychoses, character disturbances, and other pathological conditions, even including organic conditions. It remains a work frequently referred to by practicing psychoanalysts. Fenichel's approach was to identify the specific drive conflicts underlying each of the conditions discussed and then to correlate for each condition the specific drive-defense conflict with particular psychosexual developmental phases. From this matrix he offered a generalized reconstruction of the circumstances that shaped neurotic fixations during childhood.

In discussing obsessions and compulsions, for example, Fenichel argued that these phenomena may be regarded as direct or indirect manifestations of urges by drives: compulsions representing urges in behavior, obsessions representing urges in thought. For example, a child's urge to express an anal drive by touching and smearing feces comes under the control of the maturing ego system and is warded off. Its return to expression in later childhood, too, must be warded off. The warding-off process makes use of typical defenses such as isolation and reaction formation. In the case of compulsive rituals or obsessive thoughts, some people may avoid certain situations that are associated with dirt; constant vigilance then becomes necessary to assure successful avoidance. Others may become so obsessively preoccupied with avoiding dirt that "dirt" is consciously on their minds. They may feel compelled to touch some objects just so they can avoid touching other—dirty—objects, or they may feel the compulsion to wash their hands many times during the day in spite of "knowing" their hands are clean.

Fenichel discussed many varieties of compulsive symptoms, and he traced their meaning using the data of case examples and patients' free associations. Always the drive qualities and defenses against them received primary emphasis. For example, he reported:

> Overt or concealed tendencies toward cruelty or reaction formations against them are constant findings in compulsion neurosis. With equal constancy anal-erotic impulses and defenses against them are found in the most varied forms. This constant association of traits of cruelty and of anal eroticism in compulsion neuroses . . . was what convinced Freud of the close relationship of these two types of phenomena, and of the existence of an "anal sadistic" stage of libido organization. . . . The anal sadistic instinctual orientation of the compulsion neurotic can, as a rule, be easily recognized in the clinical picture, once attention has been directed to this point. Compulsion neurotics are generally and obviously concerned about conflicts between aggressiveness and submissiveness, cruelty and gentle-

ness, dirtiness and cleanliness, disorder and order. These conflicts may be expressed in the external appearance and the manifest behavior, whereas questions concerning sexual life are characteristically answered: "so far as that goes everything is in order [1945, p. 273]."

As in other neurotic reactions, regression plays a key role in compulsion neurosis. Fixations at the anal-sadistic stage of psychosexual development prepare the patient for a regressive flight from the oedipal relationships with his parents to the earlier anal-sadistic level. Fenichel offered the following case vignette, one among many:

A girl suffered from the obsessive fear that a snake might emerge from the toilet, crawl into her anus. In analysis it turned out that this fear had a forerunner: the first, phallic anxiety had been that the snake might be in her bed. To protect her from the anxiety, a regression had taken place; the location of the fear was changed from the bed to the toilet, from the genitals to the anus [1945, p. 275].

This model of psychopathology directed the psychoanalyst to the identification of the drive elements in the symptom, to the anxiety that triggered the regression to the earlier drive expression, to the nature of the drive-defense compromise, and to the reasons for the regression and the earlier fixation. But symptoms are a poor guide to the nature of psychopathology, for the same symptoms can appear in different clinical syndromes and their presence and intensity are highly variable. In the psychoanalytic view, therefore, symptoms have no fixed meaning and signifiance. Their meaning for each patient must be explored anew.

Certain groups of reactions, like hysterical, obsessional, and phobic syndromes, and certain character aberrations like those who are impulsive or some who have addictive problems seem to manifest correlated sets of impulse-defense dynamics and characteristic patterns and styles of adaptation. But there are always significant exceptions.

THE ROLE OF CHARACTER

Psychoanalysts, and particularly Freud, recognized that an explanation of psychopathology based solely on drive dynamics and defenses was incomplete, for it contained no statement about the qualities of the person showing the pathology; there was no notice taken of the contribution of the person's character and personality to the development of symptoms. Although Freud (1908), Jones (1949), and Abraham (1924) did concern themselves with an analysis of character—as enduring modes of behavior—the status of character within the theory was regarded as similar to that of symptoms: the continuation of the fate of drives. Wilhelm Reich's studies emphasized that although character had its origin in drive-defense conflicts, it had an autonomy of its own (Reich, 1949). Character qualities such as rigidity, stubbornness, ritualistic and programmed behavior are typical of those people showing compulsive symptoms. Such people are not often warm and easily approachable. For Reich these character qualities represented a solution of the childhood drive-defense conflict; thus the therapeutic focus of psychoanalysis was, in Reich's hands, to be not only on the drives and the specific defenses against them or even on the symptoms which represent their compromise, but on the syndrome of character.

THE TOTAL PERSON

In their therapeutic endeavors, most contemporary psychoanalysts rely upon many of the psychodynamic formulations of psychopathology and of Reich's additions. They regard a person's character, however, as more than the outcome of drive conflicts. Influenced by the views of Hartmann, Anna Freud, and Erikson, they recognize that while many aspects of character originate in conflict and may even continue to serve defensive functions, character seems also to have a generally adaptive function. Character would include the consistency over time of a person's typical style of employing his capacities, talents, propensities, thought, affect expression, and action. Within these consistencies, typical, characterologically determined psychopathology may develop. Thus, the choice of neurotic symptom may be traced both to the particular drive-defense dynamics and to a person's characteristic style of functioning, to his style of adaptation (cf. Shapiro, 1965).

There are comparable trends in psychosomatic medicine, that is, the study of conditions of poorly understood, complex, multidetermined etiology, such as peptic ulcer, bronchial asthma, essential hypertension, neurodermatitis, thyrotoxicosis, rheumatoid arthritis, and ulcerative colitis. The study of these conditions began with assumptions about direct correlations between specific unresolved psychological conflicts and a specific psychosomatic illness. Later, assumptions about somatic, physiological, or genetic predispositions were added. Contemporary theories acknowledge the genetic, constitutional, physiological, and complex psychological factors implicated in psychosomatic illnesses (Reiser, 1966).

A Holistic View

New clinical data continue to modify the understanding of psychopathology. Earlier oversimplifications give way to the corrective influence of experience. The psychoanalytic view of trying to understand the meaning of symptoms should not be confused with attempts to explain their genesis. Freud did not believe that the psychodynamics of neurotic conditions were sufficient explanations. Thus, the psychodynamic viewpoint of psychoanalysis is only postdictive. The economic metapsychological point of view adds a dimension to understanding, but also does not explain the cause of a psychopathological reaction. Statements about psychodynamics or psychic energy cannot imply prediction. For example, early childhood history cannot predict the future development of neurotic symptoms, psychotic reactions, sociopathic behavior, or, indeed, any discernible psychopathology. A psychoanalyst, too, must work postdictively. He studies the psychopathological reactions of an adult and from the patient's free associations about his earlier history attempts retrospectively to understand the genesis of those reactions from that particular life history.

A patient's mere understanding of the meaning of his symptoms may start him on the road to recovery, and psychoanalytic therapy may guide him on that road. But other methods of therapy may also be effective. For there is no specific cure for neurotic symptoms as there is for syphilis or pneumonia.

What should one call the psychopathology in the case of the thirty-two-year-old teacher we discussed on page 121? He began to show transvestite behavior. His work efficiency diminished; his relations with his wife deteriorated. And to complicate the picture, on one of his nightly adventures he had a homosexual liaison as a result of which he contracted a luetic infection. Now, curiously, he did not come to the psychiatrist for his syphilis, although the neurologist made the diagnosis of meningovascular syphilis. Nor did he come because of compulsive transvestite tendencies; nor for his inability to work up to his potential; nor for help in his failing marriage. He came because of pains in his legs.

One may, of course, assign multiple diagnoses to this man's condition. But in theory, wrote Karl Menninger (1948), there is no simple uncomplicated diagnosis of anything. Even a child with measles has educational, social, and familial disturbances that are part of the condition of being ill with measles. Menninger pointed out how in our everyday speech we talk about facing, warding off, or fighting illness, as if illness were something foreign to the person and not *of* him.

> The real problem is, what forces him to do it so? How have his defenses handled some new situation? And to what extent have those malignant self-destructive tendencies, which are in all of us, combined with external forces to result in pain and faltering and sometimes death [Menninger, 1959, p. 678]?

Disease, Menninger wrote, may profitably be thought of as a disturbance in a person's total functioning, a temporary imbalance between internal and external threats and pressures, on the one hand, and the organism's efforts to maintain itself via thoughts, feelings, and social relationships.

> When any one of these elements is disturbed from within or from without, the recovery of balance is attempted through a readjustment of all the others. The *agent provocateur* may be a bacterium or a bayonet, a cancer cell or a seduction, a starvation of calcium or a starvation of love. Whatever the upsetting influence, many elements cooperate to restore the balance. Sometimes they overdo it, and the last state is worse than the first. For some aspects of this imbalance we have medical terms, for some aspects we have only sociological or common speech terms. But a meaningful diagnosis cannot be confined to the terms of any one discipline. To do so is to mislabel the condition, misconceive its essential nature. What we conventionally call "disease" is sometimes the *agent provocateur,* sometimes the wound; it is sometimes the overaction of systemic defense measures and sometimes the consequence of mismanagement by relatives, friends, and even doctors. It is sometimes the picture of a triumphant malignancy, sometimes that of a quiet renunciation, a sacrifice in part for the whole, as with Polycrates' Ring. All these we have called "the disease."
> *It is the imbalance, the organismic disequilibrium, which is the real pathology,* and when that imbalance reaches a degree or duration that threatens the comfort or survival of the individual (or his environment), it may be correctly denoted disease. The protean manifestations of that im-

balance must be looked for by the doctor in all spheres of human life, identified in their relationships, understood in their totality, recognized as symptoms of the imbalance, and labeled in a pragmatically useful way. But they must never be mistaken for *"the disease"* [Menninger, 1959, p. 679].

Thus conceived, psychoanalysis provides, in Gardner Murphy's words, an epic view of human nature (Murphy, 1960). It is more than the conception of multiple determined factors in behavior, or the idea of unconscious processes that continuously influence our experience and our behavior, or the importance accorded the experiences with our patients, or the recognition of drive motivations. The psychoanalytic epic regards man as the shaper of his own fate, the forger of his own history, a being who is born to struggle against and ally himself with his inner nature and his surrounding world. In this epic, psychopathology is to be regarded not as a thing that plunders the person but as an expression of man's struggles with love and hate, life and death.

GLOSSARY

Actual neurosis: One of three neurotic syndromes: anxiety neurosis, hypochondriasis, and neurasthenia. Freud believed that the actual neuroses, in contrast to the psychoneuroses, had no psychological cause. Rather, they were physiologically caused by the accumulation of the energy of the sexual drive.

Adaptive point of view: That aspect of metapsychology which refers to the reciprocal relations between organism and environment, producing changes in both, yet not implying necessary conflict between them.

Affects: Feeling states with somatic accompaniment, such as the feeling of shame with blushing, of sadness with crying, or of fear with sweating.

Analysand: The psychoanalytic patient.

Aphonia: Loss of voice, but with the preservation of whispered speech.

Apperceptive mass: A term used by Johann Friedrich Herbart to denote the total aggregate of conscious ideas. In his theory only those ideas that "fit" with the apperceptive mass will add to its strength and become capable of achieving consciousness.

Axon: The long nerve-cell process that conducts impulses from the cell body.

Canalization: A term used by Gardner Murphy to refer to progressive developmental changes in ways of satisfying drives.

Cathartic method: A therapeutic procedure, introduced by Breuer, that aimed at releasing the expression of emotion the patient had suppressed. The method was superseded by psychoanalysis which emphasized the role of understanding in addition to that of catharsis.

Cathexis: A term derived from the Greek to denote the common German word *Bezetzung*, which means "to occupy," as an army *occupies* territory. Freud employed the term in his theory of psychic energy to indicate an investment of the sexual or aggressive drive energy in some conscious of unconscious fantasy, idea, or representation of oneself or of another person; hence the strength with which motives are held.

Censorship: An early term referring to defensive activities aimed at removing or barring some ideas from consciousness. The term was used by Freud principally in describing his model of the mind derived from an examination of dreams and dreaming.

Complementary series: A concept that takes into account the multiple etiological factors in development by including the differential and complementary weights of such variables as constitutional versus environmental factors, early versus late experiences, and fantasied versus actual experiences.

Conflict-free ego sphere: An aspect of ego functioning such as memory, concept formation, or perception, which at a particular moment is not implicated in intrapsychic conflict.

Conversion: A defense mechanism that leads to unusual alterations in body functions that resemble organic pathology, as, for example, certain paralyses or tics. Freud understood these changes to stem from unconscious fantasies whose psychic energy (libido) had been withdrawn and converted into somatic symptoms.

Countertransference: Feelings, attitudes, and fantasies, generally only partly conscious, which the analyst has toward a patient either in response to the latter's transference (q.v.) or as a reflection of the analyst's personal conflicts. Often the analyst's scrutiny of his countertransference will alert him to some of the meanings of the patient's current behavior.

Day residue: That part of a dream which represents either directly or by allusion an actual experience of real life of the day or two preceding the dream.

Dendrites: A branching or treelike process that conducts impulses toward the body of a nerve cell.

Denial: A defense mechanism which aims at the disavowal of an aspect of reality.

Developmental lines: The schedule of differentiated growth and development in several areas of sexual, aggressive, and social behavior from infancy to latency.

Displacement: A defense mechanism which consists of transferring a quantity of cathexis from a dangerous idea to an innocuous one. The result is that the previously innocuous idea receives a heightened significance while the dangerous idea loses its importance. The dangerous idea may thus remain potentially conscious.

Dream work: The mental process by which the latent dream thoughts are transformed into the manifest dream.

Drives: Forces that represent the internal motivations of behavior. In his later theorizing, Freud considered two basic innate drives, sex and aggression.

Dynamic point of view: That aspect of metapsychology which refers to drives, motives, and drive-aims and their involvement in conflict.

Economic point of view: That aspect of metapsychology which refers to the strength with which motivational aims are held.

Electroencephalograph: An apparatus for recording the electrical activity of the brain.

Energy: In physics, the capacity to do work; in psychoanalysis, the energy of the drives.

Epigenesis: Development involving gradual differentiation of an initially undifferentiated substance, affected by environmental circumstances. The concept stems from the embryology of the 1920s. In this theory, early damage to the growing entity results in greater general impairment than does later damage.

Evolution: The theory that present animal and plant species have developed by descent and modification from preexisting species.

Fantasy: A mental activity taking the form of images or ideas and representing an attempt at fulfilling a wish. Fantasies may be conscious (as in daydreams) or unconscious (as in forbidden wishes toward important people in one's life).

Fixation: The tendency for aspects of early developmental phases to acquire a dominant role in later development. In terms of the psychoanalytic energy theory, fixation represents a strong cathexis of earlier phases and early ways of controlling drive-reality conflicts, which thus acquire an excessive persistence or an attraction to which regression can more easily occur.

Functional autonomy: A term used by G. W. Allport to refer to the view that a developed behavior or attitude, while growing out of a particular motivational system, may become functionally independent of its source.

Genetic point of view: That aspect of metapsychology which focuses upon historical antecedents that appear as necessary causes of behavior.

Hypercathexis: A charge of energy added to an idea's already existing cathexis. The added investment thus imparts to the idea a sufficient "quantity" to attract the function of attention.

Identification: A mental process whereby a person changes an aspect of himself to resemble that of another person who is loved or feared. Such identifications often materialize after separations, real or symbolic.

Isolation: A defense mechanism that results in a loss of awareness of the connection of an idea with its originally associated feelings. Isolation thus permits otherwise unpleasant ideas—such as death wishes toward a parent—to remain available to consciousness because the connection is unconscious.

Latent dream thoughts: The thoughts, wishes, and attitudes that are concealed behind or within the manifest dream.

Libido: The energy of the sexual drive.

Manifest dream content: The dream as dreamed.

Metapsychology: The theoretical structure of psychoanalysis, so named by Freud because it embraced phenomena and explanations beyond those of traditional psychology of the nineteenth and early twentieth century. Metapsychology provides a framework within which mental phenomena, particularly psychopathology, may be viewed. It includes six viewpoints: adaptive, dynamic, economic, genetic, structural, and topographic.

Naturphilosophie: A romantic philosophical movement of the eighteenth and early nineteenth century—represented by such men as

Schelling, Goethe, and Schopenhauer—that emphasized intuitive rather than empirical understanding of phenomena and viewed the world in terms of basic polar conflicts.

Neuron: The fundamental functional unit of nervous tissue.

Ontogeny: The development of an individual organism.

Parapraxes: Errors such as slips of the tongue or lapses in memory.

Phylogeny: The evolutionary development of a genetically related group of organisms as distinguished from the development of an individual organism.

Pleasure principle: A presumed regulatory principle of organismic functioning. It describes the tendency of the organism to rid itself of tensions—both external and derived from drives—by the most immediate route.

Postdiction: The act of inferring probable antecedent conditions from a study of existing circumstances.

Primary autonomy: Ego functions, like memory and perception, which, in their beginning development, are relatively independent of drives and are considered inborn genesis.

Primary gain: The gratification of the infantile unconscious aim presumed to motivate neurotic symptoms.

Primary process: 1. Primitive, illogical, syncretistic, sometimes perceptually vivid thought modes. 2. Freely mobile, displaceable drive energy.

Projection: A defense mechanism whereby a painful, dangerous, or unwelcome idea is attributed to another person and felt to be directed against oneself.

Purposivism: The belief or point of view that behavior may be understood in terms of people's purposes and intentions rather than of physical analyses.

Reaction formation: A defense mechanism that results in the replacement of one set of painful or dangerous feelings by its opposite, as in the case of murderous impulses toward a loved one being replaced by oversolicitousness.

Reality principle: Modes of action and thought which take into account the reality consequences of one's actions, hence the regulation of the pleasure principle by delay and detour.

Regression: (1) A defensive retreat from a later to an earlier phase of drive development, prepared by a previous fixation. (2) A retreat from more mature to less mature adaptive or defensive functioning. (3) A retreat from ideational thinking to hallucinatory wishing.

Repression: A defense mechanism which removes from awareness a psychologically painful idea. The idea acquires its painful quality from its association with ideas that, very early in the person's life, had been connected with dangerous drive-related wishes and which had never been conscious (primal repression).

Resistance: The opposition of the analysand to free associating during a psychoanalysis. The varieties of resistance reflect the analysand's unconscious defensive activities against the recognition and expression of prohibited urges and wishes.

Secondary autonomy: Ego functions which have arisen or developed within the nexus of conflict but which subsequently have become relatively independent of drives and conflict.

Secondary gain: An added gratification—generally an interpersonal advantage—beyond that of the drives, derived from maintaining neurotic symptoms.

Secondary process: 1. Logical thinking. 2. Bound drive-energy.

Structural point of view: One of the metapsychological points of view that seeks to describe and understand mental contents and psychological behavior in terms of the functions of groups of psychological structures conceptualized as id, ego, and superego.

Topographic point of view: One of the metapsychological points of view that seeks to describe and understand mental contents in terms of their relation to consciousness.

Transference: The repetition in a current relationship of feelings, fantasies, and attitudes that were experienced originally towards significant persons such as one's parents. The process of substitution is unconscious and may occur in the course of any interpersonal relationship. When it occurs in psychoanalytic treatment, the therapeutic technique consists partly in attempts to understand and interpret the transference.

Transference neurosis: Generally, during a psychoanalysis, the patient's neurotic patterns are reexperienced within the therapeutic context, with the psychoanalyst as the central figure. Such a situation is called a transference neurosis. It provides crucial therapeutic leverage, for the patient reexperiences vividly the neurotic patterns, and that experience and the interpretation of it carry great conviction for the patient.

Turning against the self: A defense mechanism in which the object of an aggressive drive is changed from another person to the self.

Undoing: A defense mechanism in which a forbidden act is compulsively performed and then is compulsively undone, as when a hostile act is subsequently countered by propitiatory and expiatory behavior.

Zeitgeist: The general intellectual and cultural climate of taste characteristic of an era.

REFERENCES

ABRAHAM, K. (1924). The influence of oral erotism on character formation. In *Selected papers of Karl Abraham*. D. Bryan & A. Strachey (Trans.). London: Hogarth Press, 1948. Pp. 393–406.

AUGUSTINE, St. *Confessions and enchiridion*. A. C. Outler (Trans. and Ed.). Philadelphia: Westminster Press, 1955.

ALLPORT, G. *Personality*. New York: Holt, 1937.

BAILEY, P. The great psychiatric revolution. *American Journal of Psychiatry*, 1956–57, **113**, 387–406.

BERNE, E. *Games people play*. New York: Grove Press, 1964.

BERNFELD, S. Freud's earliest theories and the school of Helmholtz. *Psychoanalytic Quarterly*, 1944, **13**, 341–362.

BOLLAND, J., & SANDLER, J. *The Hampstead psychoanalytic index*. New York: International Universities Press, 1965.

BORING, E. G. Eponym as placebo. In R. I. Watson & D. T. Campbell (Eds.), *History, Psychology, and Science*. Selected papers of E. G. Boring. New York: Wiley, 1963. Pp. 5–25.

BREUER, J., & FREUD, S. (1893–1895). Studies on hysteria. *Standard edition*,[1] Vol. 2. London: Hogarth Press, 1955.

BROUN, H. *New York World-Telegram*, Sept. 26, 1939.

CHARCOT, J. M. *Lectures on the diseases of the nervous system*. London: New Sydenham Society, 1877–1889. 3 vols.

CHAPANIS, A. Men, machines, and models. *American Psychologist*, 1961, **16**, 113–131.

[1] The references to Freud's psychological writings in the *Standard edition* is to the *Standard edition of the complete psychological works of Sigmund Freud*. London: © Hogarth Press, 24 vols. Acknowledgment is also made to the other copyright holders, Sigmund Freud Copyrights Ltd. and The Institute of Psycho-Analysis, for permission to quote from the *Standard edition*.

CULLEN, W. *Synopsis nosologiae methodicae.* Edinburgh: Kincaid and Creech, 1772.

ERIKSON, E. H. *Childhood and society.* (2nd ed.). New York: W. W. Norton, 1963.

ERIKSON, E. H. *Young man Luther.* New York: W. W. Norton, 1958.

ERIKSON, E. H. On the nature of psychohistorical evidence: In search of Gandhi. *Daedalus,* Summer 1968, **97**, 695–730.

FENICHEL, O. *The psychoanalytic theory of neurosis.* New York: © W. W. Norton, 1945. Reprinted by permission.

FREUD, A. (1936). *The ego and the mechanisms of defense.* (Rev. ed.). New York: International Universities Press, 1967.

FREUD, A. *The psychoanalytic treatment of children.* New York: International Universities Press, 1946.

FREUD, A., NAGERA, H., & FREUD, W. E. Metapsychological assessment of the adult personality: The adult profile. *Psychoanalytic Study of the Child,* 1965, **20**, 9–41.

FREUD, A. The concept of developmental lines. *Psychoanalytic Study of the Child,* 1963, **18**, 245–265.

FREUD, S. Über die allgemeinwirkung des cocaïns. *Medicinisch-Chirurgisches Centralblatt,* 1885, **20**, 374–376.

Freud, S. Über den ursprung der hinteren nervenwerzeln im rückenmark von ammocoetes (petromyzon planeri). *Sitzungsberichte Der Kaiserlichen Akademie Der Wissenschaften,* 1877, 75(1):15–27.

FREUD, S. *The origins of psychoanalysis: Letters to Wilhelm Fliess, drafts and notes: 1887–1902.* (M. Bonaparte, A. Freud, & E. Kris, Eds.). New York: Basic Books, 1954.

FREUD, S. (1891). *On aphasia: a critical study.* E. Stengel (Trans.). International Universities Press, 1953.

FREUD, S. (1892–1899). Extracts from the Fliess papers. *Standard edition,* Vol. 1, 1966.

FREUD, S. (1893). On the psychical mechanism of hysterical phenomena. *Standard edition,* Vol. 3, 1962, pp. 25–39.

FREUD, S. (1894). The neuropsychoses of defense. (An attempt at a psychological theory of acquired hysteria, of many phobias and obsessions and of certain hallucinatory psychoses.) *Standard edition,* Vol. 3, 1962, pp. 43–61.

FREUD, S. (1895a). Obsessions and phobias: Their psychical mechanisms and their aetiology. *Standard edition,* Vol. 3, 1962, pp. 71–82.

FREUD, S. (1895b). On the grounds for detaching a particular syndrome from neurasthenia under the description "anxiety neurosis." *Standard edition*, Vol. 3, 1962, pp. 87–113.

FREUD, S. (1895c). Project for a scientific psychology. *Standard edition*, Vol. 1, 1966, pp. 283–387.

FREUD, S. (1896). Further remarks on the neuropsychoses of defense. *Standard edition*, Vol. 3, 1962, pp. 157–185.

FREUD, S. (1900). *The interpretation of dreams. Standard edition*, Vols. 4–5, 1953. Copyright George Allen & Unwin, Ltd., London.

FREUD, S. (1901). The psychopathology of everyday life. *Standard edition*, Vol. 6, 1960.

FREUD, S. (1905a). Fragment of an analysis of a case of hysteria. *Standard edition*, Vol. 7, pp. 7–122.

FREUD, S. (1905b). Three essays on the theory of sexuality. *Standard edition*, Vol. 7, 1953, pp. 123–320.

FREUD, S. (1906). My views on the part played by sexuality in the aetiology of the neuroses. *Standard edition*, Vol. 7, pp. 271–279.

FREUD, S. (1908). Character and anal erotism. *Standard edition*, Vol. 9, pp. 167–175.

FREUD, S. (1909). Analysis of a phobia in a five-year-old boy. *Standard edition*, Vol. 10, 1955, pp. 5–149.

FREUD, S. (1911a). Psychoanalytic notes on an autobiographical account of a case of paranoia (dementia paranoides). *Standard edition*, Vol. 12, 1958, pp. 3–82.

FREUD, S. (1911b). Formulations on the two principles of mental functioning. *Standard edition*, Vol. 12, 1958, pp. 213–226.

FREUD, S. (1913a). On beginning the treatment (further recommendations on the technique of Psychoanalysis I). *Standard edition*, Vol. 12, 1958, pp. 123–156.

FREUD, S. (1913b). Totem and taboo. *Standard edition*, Vol. 13, 1955, pp. 1–162.

FREUD, S. (1914a). Remembering, repeating and working through (further recommendations on the technique of Psychoanalysis II). *Standard edition*, Vol. 12, 1958, pp. 145–156.

FREUD, S. (1914b). On narcissism: an introduction. *Standard edition*, Vol. 14, 1957, pp. 67–102.

FREUD, S. (1914c). On the history of the psychoanalytic movement. *Standard edition*, Vol. 14, 1957, pp. 3–66.

FREUD, S. (1915). Instincts and their vicissitudes. *Standard edition*, Vol. 14, 1957, pp. 109–140.

FREUD, S. (1916–17). Introductory lectures on psychoanalysis. *Standard edition*, Vols. 15–16, 1963. Also found in Sigmund Freud's *A General Introduction to Psychoanalysis*, published by Liveright Publ. Corp., N.Y.

FREUD, S. (1917). Mourning and melancholia. *Standard edition*, Vol. 14, 1957, pp. 237–258.

FREUD, S. (1920). Beyond the pleasure principle. *Standard edition*, Vol. 18, 1955, pp. 3–64.

FREUD, S. (1923). The ego and the id. *Standard edition*, Vol. 19, 1961, pp. 3–66.

FREUD, S. (1924). Neurosis and psychosis. *Standard edition*, Vol. 19, 1961, pp. 149–153.

FREUD, S. (1926). Inhibitions, symptoms and anxiety. *Standard edition*, Vol. 20, 1959, pp. 77–175.

FREUD, S. (1927). The future of an illusion. *Standard edition*, Vol. 21, 1961, pp. 3–56.

FREUD, S. (1933). *New introductory lectures on psychoanalysis. Standard edition*, Vol. 22, 1964, pp. 3–182.

FREUD, S. (1940). An outline of psychoanalysis. *Standard edition*, Vol. 23, 1964, pp. 141–207.

GARDNER, R. W., HOLZMAN, P. S., KLEIN, G. S., LINTON, H., & SPENCE, D. P. Cognitive control. *Psychological Issues*, 1959, Monograph 4.

GRIESINGER, W. *Mental pathology in therapeutics*. C. L. Robinson and J. Rutherford (Trans.). London: New Sydenham Society, 1867. Cited by Alexander, F., and Selesnick, S. T. *The history of psychiatry*. Harper & Row, 1966. P. 152.

HARTMANN, H. (1939). *Ego psychology and the problem of adaptation*. David Rapaport (Trans.). New York: International Universities Press, 1958.

HARTMANN, H. Comments on the psychoanalytic theory of the ego. *Psychoanalytic Study of the Child*, 1950, 5, 74–96.

HARTMANN, H., KRIS, E., & LOEWENSTEIN, R. Comments on the formation of psychic structure. *Psychoanalytic Study of the Child*, 1946, 2, 11–38.

HERBART, J. F. *A textbook in psychology*. New York: Appleton, 1891.

HOLT, R. R. Two influences upon Freud's scientific thought: A fragment of intellectual biography. In R. W. White (Ed.), *The study of lives, essays on personality in honor of Henry A. Murray.* New York: Atherton, 1963. Pp. 364–387.

HOLZMAN, P. S.   On procrastinating. *International Journal of Psychoanalysis*, 1964, **45**, 98–109.

HUME, D.   *An enquiry concerning human understanding.* Chicago, Open Court, 1901.

JACKSON, J. H.   (1931).   In James Taylor (Ed.), *Selected writings of John Hughlings Jackson.* London: Hodder and Stoughton. 2 vols.

JANET, P.   *L'automatisme psychologique.* (2nd ed.) Vol. 21. Paris: F. Alcan, 1894.

JONES, E.   Anal-erotic character traits. In *Papers on psychoanalysis.* (5th ed.). Williams and Wilkins, 1949. Pp. 413–437.

JONES, E.   *The life and work of Sigmund Freud.* Vol. 1. New York: Basic Books, 1953.

KLEIN, G. S.   Consciousness in psychoanalytic theory: Some implications for current research in perception. *Journal of the American Psychoanalytic Association*, 1959, **7**, 5–34.

KLEIN, M.   *The psychoanalysis of children.* A. Strachey (Trans.). London: Hogarth Press, 1963.

KOHUT, H.   Forms and transformations of narcissism. *Journal of the American Psychoanalytic Association*, 1966, **14**, 243–277.

KOHUT, H.   The psychoanalytic treatment of narcissistic personality disorders: Outline of a systematic approach. *Psychoanalytic study of the child*, 1968, **23**, 86–113.

LEIBNIZ, G. W.   *Philosophical papers and letters.* Chicago: University of Chicago Press, 1956. 2 vols.

MAURY, L. F. A.   De certains faits observés dans les rêves et dans l'état interne entre le sommeil et la veille. *Annales Medico-Psychologiques.* 3d. ser. 3:157–176, 1857.

MEEHL, P.   A psychoanalyst and a methodologist look at two examples of psychoanalytic research. Paper presented at the American Psychological Association meeting, New York, September 1966.

MENNINGER, K.   Changing concepts of disease. *Annals of Internal Medicine*, **29**, 318–325, August 1948 and in *A psychiatrist's world: The Selected papers of Karl Menninger.* New York: Viking Press, 1959. Pp. 670–679.

MENNINGER, K.   (WITH MAYMAN, M. & PRUYSER, P.).   *The vital balance.* New York: Viking Press, 1963.

MURPHY, G. *Historical introduction to modern psychology.* New York: Harcourt, Brace, 1949.

MURPHY, G. Psychoanalysis as a unified theory of social behavior. In J. H. Masserman (Ed.), *Psychoanalysis and human values.* New York: Grune & Stratton, 1960. Pp. 140–149.

MURPHY, G. *Personality.* (2nd ed.) New York: Basic Books, 1966.

NAGERA, H. *Early childhood disturbances, the infantile neurosis, and the adult disturbances.* New York: International Universities Press, 1966.

OPPENHEIMER, R. Analogy in science. *American Psychologist,* 1956, **11**, 127–135.

PENFIELD, W., & ROBERTS, L. *Speech and brain-mechanisms.* Princeton: Copyright © Princeton University Press, 1959.

PIAGET, J. *The origins of intelligence in children.* New York: International Universities Press, 1952.

PIERS, G., & SINGER, M. B. *Shame and guilt: A psychoanalytic and a cultural study.* Springfield, Illinois: Charles C Thomas, 1953.

RAPAPORT, D. The structure of psychoanalytic theory: A systematizing attempt. *Psychological Issues,* 1960, Monograph 6.

RAPAPORT, D. *Collected papers of David Rapaport.* Merton M. Gill (Ed.). New York: Basic Books, 1967.

RAPAPORT, D., & GILL, M. M. The points of view and assumptions of metapsychology. In *Collected papers of David Rapaport.* New York: Basic Books, 1967. Pp. 795–811.

RAPAPORT, D., GILL, M. M., & SCHAFER, R. *Diagnostic psychological testing.* (Rev. ed.). Robert R. Holt (Ed.). New York: International Universities Press, 1968.

REICH, W. *Character analysis.* (3rd ed.). New York: Noonday, 1949.

REISE, W. History and principles of classification of nervous diseases. *History of medicine,* 1945, **18**, 465–512.

REISER, M. F. Toward an integrated psychoanalytic-physiological theory of psychosomatic disorders. In *Psychoanalysis: a general psychology.* New York: International Universities Press, 1966. Pp. 570–582.

SANDLER, J. On the concept of the superego. *Psychoanalytic study of the child,* 1960, **15**, 128–162.

SANDLER, J., & NAGERA, H. Aspects of the metapsychology of fantasy. *Psychoanalytic study of the child,* 1963, **18**, 159–194.

SANDLER, J., & ROSENBLATT, B. The concept of the representational world. *Psychoanalytic study of the child*, 1962, **17**, 128–145.

SCHAFER, R. The loving and beloved superego in Freud's structural theory. *Psychoanalytic study of the child*, 1960, **15**, 163–188.

SCHAFER, R. *Aspects of internalization*. New York: International Universities Press, 1968.

SCHEERER, M. Problems of performance analysis in the study of personality. *Annals of the N.Y. academy of sciences*, 1945–1946, **46**, 653–678.

SHAPIRO, D. *Neurotic styles*. New York: Basic Books, 1965.

SPRENGER, J., & KRAMER, H. *Malleus malificarum*. M. Summers (Trans. & Ed.). London: Pushkin Press, 1948.

WAELDER, R. The problem of the genesis of psychical conflict in earliest infancy. *International Journal of Psychoanalysis*, 1937, **18**, 406–473.

WAELDER, R. *Basic theory of psychoanalysis*. New York: International Universities Press, 1960.

WERNER, H. *Comparative psychology of mental development*. Chicago: Follett, 1948.

WEYER, J. *De praestigiis daemonum, et incantationibus, ac veneficiis*, Libri V. Basileae: Per Joannem Oporinum, 1563.

WHITE, R. Ego and reality in psychoanalytic theory. *Psychological Issues*, 1963, Monograph 11.

INDEX

INDEX